WALKING RÙM AND THE SMALL ISLES

RÙM, EIGG, MUCK, CANNA

By Peter Edwards and Katie Featherstone

JUNIPER HOUSE, MURLEY MOSS,
OXENHOLME ROAD, KENDAL, CUMBRIA LA9 7RL
www.cicerone.co.uk

© Peter Edwards and Katie Featherstone 2025
Second edition 2025

ISBN: 978 1 78631 217 4
eISBN: 978 1 78765 220 0
First edition 2012

Cicerone's EU representative for GPSR compliance is Easy Access System Europe, Mustamäe tee 50, 10621 Tallinn, Estonia. Email gpsr.requests@easproject.com.

Printed in the UK by 4edge using responsibly sourced paper.
A catalogue record for this book is available from the British Library.
All photographs are by the authors unless otherwise stated.
© Crown copyright and database rights 2025 OS AC0000810376

Updates to this guide

While every effort is made by our authors to ensure the accuracy of guidebooks as they go to print, changes can occur during the lifetime of an edition. Any updates that we know of for this guide will be on the Cicerone website (www.cicerone.co.uk/1217/updates), so please check before planning your trip. We also advise that you check information about such things as transport, accommodation and shops locally. Even rights of way can be altered over time. We are always grateful for information about any discrepancies between a guidebook and the facts on the ground, sent by email to updates@cicerone.co.uk.

Register your book: To sign up to receive free updates, special offers and GPX files where available, create a Cicerone account and register your purchase via the 'My Account' tab at www.cicerone.co.uk.

Front cover: Looking on to the cliffs beneath Beinn Tighe, Canna (Walk 21)

CONTENTS

Route summary table 6

INTRODUCTION 11
When to go 13
Getting there 14
Maps and route-finding 14
Access 16
Safety and emergencies 17
What to take. 19
Using this guidebook 20

RÙM 21
Walk 1: A round of the Rùm Cuillin 34
Walk 2: The Dibidil Horseshoe. 40
Walk 3: Askival and Hallival from Kinloch 44
Walk 4: Hallival and Barkeval from Kinloch 48
Walk 5: Around the coast of Rùm. 54
Day 1: Kinloch to Dibidil 56
Day 2: Dibidil to Guirdil 60
Day 3: Guirdil to Kinloch 67
Walk 6: Kinloch to Guirdil 74
Walk 7: The Guirdil Horseshoe. 79
Walk 8: Orval and Àrd Nev 83
Walk 9: Kinloch to Harris Bay 87
Walk 10: Kinloch to Kilmory Bay 91
Walk 11: Port na Caranean. 94

EIGG 97
Walk 12: Uamh Fhraing and Uamh Chràbhaichd. 108
Walk 13: Grulin from Galmisdale. 112
Walk 14: An Sgùrr and Grulin 115
Walk 15: Beannan Breaca and the south-west 119
Walk 16: The Beinn Bhuidhe plateau from Galmisdale. 124
Walk 17: Sgorr an Fhàraidh 129
Walk 18: Camas Sgiotaig and the north-west coast. 132
Walk 19: Around the north-east coast of Eigg 135

CANNA AND SANDAY 141
Walk 20: A' Chill, Compass Hill and Black Sand Beach 150
Walk 21: Around Canna. 154
Walk 22: Around Sanday 161

MUCK 165
Walk 23: Around Muck 173
Walk 24: Beinn Airein and Camas Mòr. 179
Walk 25: Caisteal an Dùin Bhàin and the far south coast 183

Appendix A: Useful websites 186
Appendix B: Further reading 187

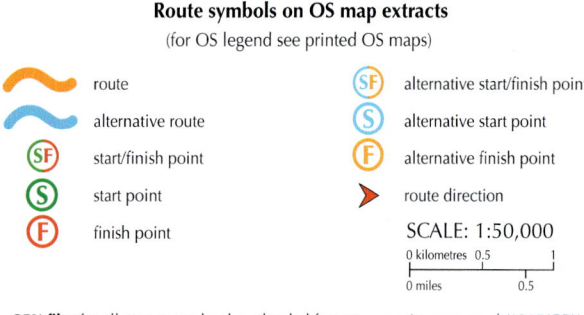

Acknowledgements

Peter

Katie Featherstone is a force of nature and I'm mighty pleased she agreed to take on the second edition of this book, which she has improved immeasurably. Along with the team at Cicerone of course!

Rhenigidale's very own Kirsty MacKay was my fixer and walking companion – along with Poppy and Ruadh – for the 'fieldwork' trips to Rùm.

On previous visits to Rùm and the Small Isles I have very much enjoyed the company of Kirsten Abingdon, Rich Baldwin, Sarah Blann, James Boulter, Andy and Jen Dodd, Clare Meadows, Fiona Rintoul and Dougal Mòr.

Thanks to the lovely Fiona for maintaining her sense of humour as we approach our twentieth year together.

Katie

Predominantly, I would like to thank Peter, who not only wrote the first edition of this book and asked me to be involved in this one, but also serves as a much-needed friend and colleague in the often-isolating world of freelance writing. Additionally, thank you to everyone at Cicerone for the warm welcome, and to the Small Isles' residents who have helped me enormously over the course of researching several guidebooks – particularly to Isebail MacKinnon, Tamsin and Stuart McCarthy, and Ruth MacEwen for hosting me. At home, on the somewhat bigger Isle of Islay, I remain grateful to my husband Dan for supporting both me and my unlucrative career choices, my family for tempting us to move to the Hebrides, and the rest of our loved ones for doing their best to keep in touch despite the distance between us.

ROUTE SUMMARY TABLE

Walk	Title	Start	Finish	Distance	Ascent	Time	Page
Rùm							
1	A round of the Rùm Cuillin	Kinloch NM 402 997	Kinloch NM 402 997	23.8km (14.8 miles)	2025m (6645ft)	9–10hr	34
2	The Dibidil Horseshoe	Dibidil bothy NM 393 927	Dibidil bothy NM 393 927	10.5km (6.5 miles)	1530m (5020ft)	5–6hr	40
3	Askival and Hallival from Kinloch	Kinloch NM 402 997	Kinloch NM 402 997	11.8km (7.3 miles)	1010m (3315ft)	5–6hr	44
4	Hallival and Barkeval from Kinloch	Kinloch NM 402 997	Kinloch NM 402 997	11.3km (7 miles)	825m (2705ft)	4–5hr	48
5	Around the coast of Rùm	Dibidil pony path NM 404 991	Kinloch NM 402 997	41.6km (25.8 miles)	2210m (7250ft)	3 days	54
6	Kinloch to Guirdil	Kinloch NM 402 997	Guirdil NG 319 013	10.5km (6.5 miles) each way	415m (1360ft)	3hr 30min–4hr each way	74
7	The Guirdil Horseshoe	Guirdil NG 319013	Guirdil NG 319 013	10.9km (6.8 miles)	888m (2915ft)	3hr 30min–4hr 30min	79
8	Orval and Àrd Nev	Kinloch NM 402 997	Kinloch NM 402 997	19.5km (12.1 miles)	850m (2790ft)	6–6hr 30min	83
9	Kinloch to Harris Bay	Kinloch NM 402 997	Kinloch NM 402 997	21.5km (13.4 miles)	670m (2200ft)	5–6hr 30min	87

Route summary table

Walk	Title	Start	Finish	Distance	Ascent	Time	Page
10	Kinloch to Kilmory Bay	Kinloch NM 402 997	Kinloch NM 402 997	16km (9.9 miles)	380m (1245ft)	5–5hr 30min	91
11	Port na Caranean	Kinloch ferry pier NM 402 997	Kinloch ferry pier NM 402 997	3.3km (2 miles)	100m (330ft)	1hr 30min–2hr	94

Eigg

Walk	Title	Start	Finish	Distance	Ascent	Time	Page
12	Uamh Fhraing and Uamh Chràbhaichd	Galmisdale pier NM 484 838	Galmisdale pier NM 484 838	3.5km (2.2 miles)	150m (490ft)	1hr 15min	108
13	Grulin from Galmisdale	Galmisdale pier NM 484 838	Galmisdale pier NM 484 838	9km (5.6 miles)	200m (655ft)	2–3hr	112
14	An Sgùrr and Grulin	Galmisdale pier NM 484 838	Galmisdale pier NM 484 838	11.5km (7.1 miles)	415m (1360ft)	4–5hr	115
15	Beannan Breaca and the south-west	Galmisdale pier NM 484 838	Galmisdale pier NM 484 838	17.8km (11 miles)	475m (1560ft)	6–7hr	119
16	The Beinn Bhuidhe plateau from Galmisdale	Galmisdale pier NM 484 838	Galmisdale pier NM 484 838	17.5km (10.9 miles)	430m (1410ft)	7–8hr 30min	124
17	Sgorr an Fhàraidh	Cleadale War Memorial NM 477 887	Cleadale War Memorial NM 477 887	6.3km (3.9 miles)	305m (1000ft)	1hr 30min–2hr 30min	129
18	Camas Sgiotaig and the north-west coast	Cleadale war memorial NM 477 887	Cleadale war memorial NM 477 887	6km (3.7 miles)	160m (525ft)	1hr 30min–2hr	132
19	Around the north-east coast of Eigg	Cleadale war memorial NM 477 887	Cleadale war memorial NM477887	14.8km (9.2 miles)	500m (1640ft)	6–7hr	135

Walk	Title	Start	Finish	Distance	Ascent	Time	Page
Canna and Sanday							
20	A' Chill, Compass Hill and Black Sand Beach	Canna community shop NG 275 055	Canna community shop NG 275 055	4km (2.5 miles)	125m (410ft)	1–2hr	150
21	Around Canna	Canna community shop NG 275 055	Canna community shop NG 275 055	20km (12.4 miles)	605m (1985ft)	7–9hr	154
22	Around Sanday	Canna–Sanday bridge NG 266 050	Canna–Sanday bridge NG 266 050	9.3km (5.8 miles)	125m (410ft)	3–4hr	161
Muck							
23	Around Muck	The old pier, Port Mòr NM 422 793	The old pier, Port Mòr NM 422 793	14.8km (9.2 miles)	300m (985ft)	4hr 30min–6hr	173
24	Beinn Airein and Camas Mòr	Gallanach NM 409 802	Gallanach NM 409 802	5km (3.1 miles)	150m (490ft)	1hr 30min–2hr 30min	179
25	Caisteal an Dùin Bhàin	The old pier, Port Mòr NM 422 793	The old pier, Port Mòr NM 422 793	4.5km (2.8 miles)	80m (260ft)	1–2hr	183

Mountain safety

Every mountain walk has its dangers, and those described in this guidebook are no exception. All who walk or climb in the mountains should recognise this and take responsibility for themselves and their companions along the way. The authors and publisher have made every effort to ensure that the information contained in this guide was correct when it went to press, but, except for any liability that cannot be excluded by law, they cannot accept responsibility for any loss, injury or inconvenience sustained by any person using this book.

International distress signal *(emergency only)*
Six blasts on a whistle (and flashes with a torch after dark) spaced evenly for one minute, followed by a minute's pause. Repeat until an answer is received. The response is three signals per minute followed by a minute's pause.

Helicopter rescue
The following signals are used to communicate with a helicopter:

Help needed: raise both arms above head to form a 'Y'

Help not needed: raise one arm above head, extend other arm downward

Emergency telephone number
999

Weather reports
The Mountain Weather Information Service (MWIS) www.mwis.org.uk

Mountain rescue can be very expensive – be adequately insured.

Hallival seen from the Coire nan Grunnd (Walk 5)

INTRODUCTION

Looking across Loch nam Ban Mòra to the Rùm Cuillin (Walk 14)

Rùm, Eigg, Muck and Canna, the wild, rugged and beautiful islands comprising the Small Isles archipelago, lie scattered off mainland Scotland's Atlantic coast, north of Ardnamurchan, west of Morar, south of Skye and east of the Outer Hebridean isles of Barra and South Uist.

The Small Isles are grouped together because of their geographic proximity, but each of these islands has a distinctive character of its own. Rùm has its towering, volcanic Cuillin hills, magnificent glens and corries and a coastline that is by turns forbiddingly rugged and breathtakingly beautiful.

The Isle of Eigg is crowned by the remarkable pitchstone crest of An Sgùrr, standing sentinel over the island, while the sweeping curve of Laig Bay and the scattered township of Cleadale are backed by the imposing basalt cliffs flanking the Beinn Bhuide plateau.

Canna, northernmost of the island group, is principally formed of tiered volcanic rock rising to twin plateaux, flanked by a rampart of awe-inspiring cliffs, which are joined by a low-lying isthmus and skirted by a raised shore

Dùn Mòr sea stack, Sanday (Walk 22)

platform. Accessible by bridge, its smaller, tide-separated sibling, Sanday has its formidable sea stacks, which host puffins in the summer months. Canna and Sanday's settlements fringe the sheltered deep-water anchorage in the island's lee.

The fertile, low-lying Isle of Muck is the smallest of the Small Isles by some margin. Beyond the main settlement at Port Mòr, much of the land is given over to a single family-run livestock farm, which lends the island a pleasant bucolic atmosphere. Indeed, when the weather is fine there can be few Scottish islands as idyllic as Muck. The fascinating coastline with its tremendous views lends itself to relaxed exploration on foot.

Each of the Small Isles is home to abundant wildlife as well as small, but tenacious island communities. Geography, geology, human and natural history all shape these islands and, without doubt, walking is the best way to experience their remarkable landscapes.

The Small Isles are often referred to as the 'hidden gems' of the Hebrides – and with good cause. Although these islands don't lack for magnificent and dramatic landscapes of their own, they tend to be overlooked, literally and metaphorically, by the numerous visitors drawn to the famously scenic grandeur of the neighbouring Isle of Skye. While Skye has a convenient road bridge, the

Small Isles' relative dearth of visitors is compounded by logistical challenges. The ferry service is fairly sparse, and there are few roads or metalled tracks; visitors are not usually allowed to bring vehicles. Although the islands' amenities are generally excellent, they are far from extensive, so organising supplies also requires a little forethought.

While some visitors are deterred by these factors, there are considerable upsides to choosing the Small Isles for a walking trip. The near non-existent vehicle traffic comes as a welcome relief, and there is the real sense of space found among the hills or along the rugged coastlines and beach-garlanded shores. These wonderful islands are a haven for those who like to get away from the madding crowd and enjoy the peace and freedom of walking through landscapes unaffected by large-scale tourism.

The Small Isles are so named for an obvious reason – Rùm, the largest of the group, is just 14km north to south by 13.5km east to west. Yet this relatively small archipelago offers remarkable scope for the adventurous walker, providing a range of fine and varied walking, from the formidable peaks of the Rùm Cuillin to the low-lying coastline of the diminutive Isle of Muck. Indeed, many of the routes in this guidebook are coastal walks taking in some remarkably varied terrain, from rugged, rocky shores and vertiginous cliffs to expanses of flower-carpeted machair and white shell-sand beaches.

These coastal landscapes teem with wildlife, and with remarkable geological features, including raised beaches, caves, natural arches, sea stacks and basalt dikes. Many traces of the islands' histories, both ancient and more recent, are found around these coastlines, from Bronze Age duns (fortifications) perched on rocky promontories to long-abandoned settlements bearing mute testament to the legacy of the Highland Clearances.

Given the relative size of the island and the range of excellent walking available, Rùm is the main focus of this guidebook, although Eigg, Canna and Muck are also comprehensively covered. Extensive sections on the fascinating geology, history and wildlife are included within each island section.

WHEN TO GO

In late spring, summer and early autumn you are more likely to benefit from mild weather. May and June tend to be the finest months, although rain – often torrential – can be a feature at any time of year. During the milder months the highly aggressive island midge abounds in alarming numbers on Rùm and Eigg; less so on the breezier, lower-lying isles of Canna and Muck. Deer ticks are also most active in warmer weather.

If properly protected against rain, midges and ticks (see 'What to take'), late spring through to autumn provides the longest days, useful if you're attempting a round of the Rùm Cuillin or when staying in remote bothies. The summer ferry timetable is more accommodating, services are less prone to weather-related cancellations, and a wider range of island amenities are open. Obviously, there are more visitors at these times of year so you're more likely to encounter other walkers, and the bothies and bays are also visited by intrepid sea-kayakers.

In winter you're almost guaranteed to have the islands' hinterlands to yourself, but the days are short and wild weather is a strong possibility. But it can be surprisingly mild in winter, thanks to the benign influence of the Gulf Stream, and – if you're lucky – you might enjoy some of those priceless, crystal-clear, sunlit winter days, as well as star-studded dark nights and the possibility of auroras. The terrain can be very boggy in winter, with December and January being the wettest months on the islands; crossing burns and rivers can be hazardous when they are in spate after heavy rain. In winter, it is especially important to ensure you are properly equipped for the conditions and let others know your planned route before setting out.

GETTING THERE

Caledonian MacBrayne (Mallaig office tel 01687 462403 calmac.co.uk) operates the principal ferry service from Mallaig to Rùm and the Small Isles. Foot passengers are advised to book in advance, while vehicle tickets are not sold without special permission; this is usually only granted to residents, people working on the islands or – in certain cases – disabled Blue Badge holders.

Each sailing usually visits multiple islands, which can make the frequently updated timetable (found online) confusing to read. In summer, each island has five or six crossings per week; this number is reduced to three or four in winter. Journey times depend on which island is visited first: a direct ferry to Rùm takes 1hr 25min, while sailing to Canna via two other islands can take over 4hr. Visiting multiple islands in one trip is entirely possible and worthwhile, but does require careful examination of the timetable in advance. There is a potential for ferries to be cancelled due to weather at any time, but it happens more frequently between September and March.

An additional passenger ferry service is run by Arisaig Marine (tel 01687 450224 www.arisaig.co.uk), which operates the *MV Sheerwater* between Arisaig and the Small Isles during the summer months.

AquaXplore (tel 01471 866244 www.aquaxplore.co.uk) also operate a fast RIB (rigid inflatable boat) service from Elgol on Skye to the Small Isles.

MAPS AND ROUTE-FINDING

This guidebook includes detailed descriptions of 25 coastal and hill

MAPS AND ROUTE-FINDING

An Coroghon and Black Sand Beach with the east end of Sanday and Rùm in the distance (Walk 20)

routes on these often rugged and sublimely beautiful islands. These are predominantly demanding routes in terms of the terrain, the distance covered or both. The terrain is extremely varied and often challenging, but the rewards are plentiful, as these routes traverse some breathtakingly beautiful scenery alive with a profusion of plants and wildlife and full of historical interest. There are few waymarks, signposts or paths of any kind, making accurate route finding and a degree of navigational proficiency indispensable.

It is essential that you have the appropriate maps to accompany the routes. This guidebook incorporates 1:50,000 mapping with highlighted routes, which should be used in conjunction with OS Explorer and Harvey Maps 1:25,000 maps because of their greater topographic detail. Do not rely solely on the maps in this guidebook as it is essential that you are able to ascertain your position in the wider context, should you need to abandon your walk and make for the nearest road or habitation. The walks described in this guidebook are covered by the following maps:

- OS Explorer 1:25,000 sheet 397 Rùm, Eigg, Muck, Canna and Sanday

Walking Rùm and the Small Isles

Red deer stag with antlers in velvet, Guirdil

- OS Landranger 1:50,000 sheet 39 Rùm, Eigg, Muck and Canna
- Harvey Maps 1:25,000 Rùm, Eigg, Canna, Muck Superwalker XT25

A compass and/or GPS system is indispensable and an altimeter is also very useful for navigation, especially on the hills of Rùm. It's not quite so easy to get lost when walking along the coast, but it is important that you know exactly where you are as impassible obstacles may be encountered – even on the smallest islands. Careful navigation becomes especially vital in poor weather or visibility; if for any reason you need to alter your course; or in an emergency situation, so you can inform rescue services of your precise location.

ACCESS

The Land Reform (Scotland) Act 2003 established legal right of non-motorised public access over most land and inland water in Scotland. The Act is supported by the Scottish Outdoor Access Code. In effect, the Act means that walkers have the right to roam, but should exercise that right in ways which are compatible with land management needs. Forestry, deerstalking, grouse shooting, lambing and other farming and crofting practices are the activities most liable to restrict walkers' movements. This is as much the case in the Hebrides as in the Highlands. Forestry is limited to the area around Kinloch on Rùm and some patches of Eigg's southern interior.

Rùm is the only island with a deer population and, consequently, deerstalking. The stalking season runs from mid-August to mid-February; however, NatureScot advises that there are no restrictions to access for walkers during this period but urges hillwalkers to check online for deer-stalking information before setting out (www.nature.scot/search?query=stalking). Between March and May it is important to avoid disturbing sheep during lambing. Avoiding interference with other farming and crofting practices is usually manageable with minimal inconvenience.

Wild camping is permitted but please check the Outdoor Access Code (www.outdooraccess-scotland.scot) for information about your rights and responsibilities.

SAFETY AND EMERGENCIES

Safety

In fine weather the Inner Hebrides can seem like an earthly paradise; however, the onset of high winds and driving rain can rapidly make the place feel quite hellish, especially if you are exposed to the elements. It is essential that you are properly equipped and able to navigate proficiently when visibility is poor. Check the weather forecast before setting out and allow yourself plenty of time to complete your day's itinerary during daylight. Always let someone know your intended route and estimated time of completion. Carry a first-aid kit, survival blanket, mobile phone and plenty of food. Carry spare layers and wear at least one item of high-visibility clothing. A whistle and/or torch are important for attracting attention in case of injury. Six blasts on the whistle or six torch flashes should be repeated every minute. Consider carrying a personal locator beacon (PLB; see Emergencies, below), especially if you are on your own and/or walking in a remote area where mobile phone coverage may be patchy or non-existent.

Only fit, properly equipped, experienced hillwalkers with reliable navigation skills should attempt a round

A Calmac ferry in Port Mòr (Walks 23 and 25)

of the Rùm Cuillin – and then only in good conditions. The weather can change rapidly in this maritime mountain environment. The terrain is difficult in places and visibility can be lost with little warning. After heavy rain or snowfall many burns and rivers run very high, with a terrific volume of fast-moving water. This is especially the case on mountainous Rùm. Do not attempt to cross rivers in spate – if you are swept away your chances of survival are very small. If you're successful in crossing one river in such conditions you may come up against an impassable torrent further on; if you then attempt to recross the river you previously crossed, you may find that it is running higher and faster than before.

Emergencies

In case of injury or other incident, it is important to stay calm and assess your situation. Try to ascertain your exact position on the map and consider your options for walking to safety, finding shelter, staying put or seeking help. Remember that it may take an emergency team some hours to reach you, especially in poor conditions in a remote area. Mountain Rescue in the UK hills is undertaken by volunteers – albeit working at a high level of professionalism – who, without payment,

Port Chreadhain near Gallanach with Rùm in the distance (Walk 23)

help save lives while risking their own. They are organised and assisted by the police.

Before you set off, register your phone with emergency SMS, and understand how this system works: go to www.relayuk.bt.com and select 'How to use Relay UK', then 'Contact 999 using Relay UK'.

Make sure your phone is protected from water and be aware that colder temperatures outdoors can drain the battery; switch the device off or keep on flight mode unless you need it, and carry a separate power bank as backup.

You may also consider carrying a personal locator beacon (PLB). This is an electronic transmitting device that, once activated, will alert rescue services to a life-threatening situation in the air, on water or in remote areas. If you or a companion is injured and you need to call for help, **call 999 and ask for Police, then Mountain Rescue**. Then give the following details:
- Location (with a grid reference if possible)
- Name, gender and age of the casualty
- Nature of injuries or emergency
- Number of people in the group
- Your mobile phone number

Then, stay where you are until you are found.

WHAT TO TAKE

The OS Explorer 1:25,000 or Harvey Superwalker maps are indispensable (a waterproof map case is advisable), as is a compass and/or GPS device. An altimeter is also very useful. A robust rucksack with adequate capacity and a comfortable harness is indispensable. For day walks, a 30+ litre pack should be sufficient; for longer trips, when you are carrying camping gear and several days' food, a 60+ litre pack may be required. Effective waterproofs (jacket and trousers) are essential when undertaking a walk of any length in the Hebrides. Use a waterproof pack liner inside your rucksack, and add a second layer of protection – made-for-purpose dry bags are the best option – for vulnerable electronics, as well as any dry clothes or a sleeping bag. Weather can change quickly on the islands and doesn't always obey the forecasts.

Lightweight, 'wickable', quick drying clothing is a must when walking the often-strenuous routes in this guide. Carry adequate warm clothing: extra layers are useful when you take breaks. The nature of much of the terrain – on Rùm, Eigg and Canna especially – requires robust walking boots with ankle support and a Vibram sole.

It is difficult to keep your feet dry at the best of times when walking on the islands, so Gore-Tex-lined or well-waxed boots are essential. Gaiters provide protection from boggy ground and rough undergrowth, while telescopic walking poles are very useful, especially when carrying a heavy pack on multi-day walks. A warm hat and gloves should find a place in your rucksack, even in summer. Sun cream, a sun hat and sunglasses should also be carried from spring through to autumn and lip balm is also useful.

Always carry plenty of food, including high-energy snacks, and make sure you have enough water. With the exceptions of Muck and Sanday, there are frequent opportunities to fill up from the islands' many burns. The water is generally safe to drink; however, be careful around livestock and take water-purifying tablets if you are worried about contamination. A mobile phone is essential in case of misadventure, and a power bank can provide additional battery reserves. A basic medical kit and a survival blanket should always be carried, and a head torch is invaluable if you are benighted; the latter can help to attract attention in an emergency, and carrying a whistle is useful for the same purpose. From late spring until late autumn it is worth carrying some serious insect repellent (some swear by Avon 'Skin So Soft') and a midge/mosquito hat – or net to place over a hat – is a useful line of defence against *Culicoides impunctatus*. Patent tick tweezers or tick-removing forks are the best tools for this delicate job. Lightweight binoculars are worth their weight for admiring the islands' splendid wildlife.

USING THIS GUIDEBOOK

The routes in this guide are grouped by island into four sections, each preceded by an overview map. Separate island introductions cover the local geology, history, wildlife, transport and amenities. The walks are described in some detail and illustrated with extracts from the 1:50,000 maps. For each route, the distance, rough timing, ascent, terrain, difficulty and corresponding OS or Harvey map you will need to carry with you are listed, alongside the grid reference for your start and finish points. The appendices at the end of the book include useful websites and suggestions for further reading.

GPX tracks

GPX tracks for the routes in this guidebook are available to download free at www.cicerone.co.uk/1217/GPX. A GPS device is an excellent aid to navigation, but you should also carry a map and compass and know how to use them. GPX files are provided in good faith, but in view of the profusion of formats and devices, neither the author nor the publisher accepts responsibility for their use.

RÙM

Beneath Hallival's rugged northwest face (Walk 4)

Askival, Ainshval and Trollabhal from the Bealach Bairc-Mheall (Walks 1, 3 and 4)

RÙM

Rùm is by far the largest of the Small Isles with an area of 100km² and, at 14km north to south by 13.5km east to west, it is the 15th largest of the Scottish islands. It is the wettest and arguably the most mountainous island of its size in Britain. Its striking profile of jagged basalt and gabbro mountain peaks testifies to its volcanic origins. Rùm's highest peaks, Askival (812m) and Ainshval (781m), are Corbetts – those Scottish mountains between 2500 and 3000ft (762m and 914m) with a relative height of at least 500ft (152m): Rùm is the smallest Scottish island to have a summit over 2500ft (762m).

Kinloch, the island's only settlement, lies at the head of Loch Scresort, the main anchorage, some 27km west of the mainland ferry port of Mallaig and the Morar peninsula. Rùm is 11km south of Skye at its nearest point and 23km north-west of the Ardnamurchan peninsula. The island has a tiny population – around 40 people – and when the village of Kinloch is left behind a true sense of wildness is soon found amid the island's dramatic and sometimes challenging landscapes. The only other habitations, besides the bothies at Dibidil and Guirdil, are the red deer research base at Kilmory Bay and the NatureScot lodge at Harris Bay.

The distinctive volcanic chain of hills comprising the Rùm Cuillin is the obvious and immediate draw for outdoor enthusiasts, whether for hillwalking, scrambling or rock climbing. A round of the Rùm Cuillin makes for a challenging day in the hills and usually features somewhere on the 'to-do' list of Scottish mountain aficionados. But for the adventurous walker there is much more to Rùm than the Cuillin alone. This guidebook includes detailed route descriptions for several major walks – including a three-day walk around the coast and circular routes around the remote western hills – as well as a number of less-challenging routes.

Landrover tracks cross the island from Kinloch to Kilmory and Harris, and there are several long-established footpaths, including the well-worn track up alongside the Allt Slugan to the Coire Dubh – gateway to the Rùm Cuillin – and the pony path around the coast from Kinloch to Dibidil bothy and Papadil. Other areas lack distinct paths, necessitating detailed route descriptions and mapping – all the more so as Rùm is exceptionally prone to cloud cover, with associated implications for navigation. Walking conditions on Rùm are often wet and rough: it

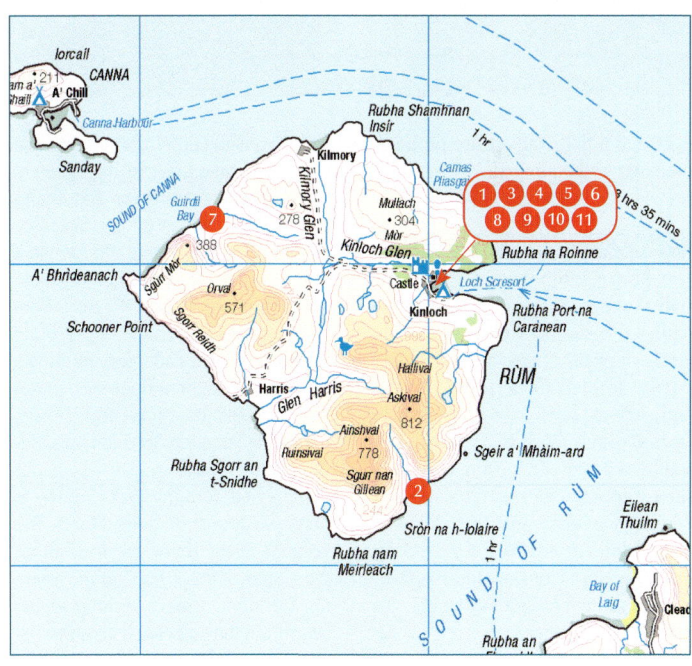

Pillow lava outcrop near Glen Shellesder (Walks 5 and 6)

is essential that walkers are properly prepared and equipped.

GEOLOGY

The Rùm Cuillin form the impressive skyline of jagged peaks dominating the south of the island. The northern peaks of the range are principally formed of peridotite basalt and gabbro, similar in construction to the Black Cuillin of Skye. The southern peaks are Torridonian sandstone capped with quartz-felsite and Lewisian gneiss, and the rounded granite hills of Àrd Nev, Orval, Sròn an t-Saighdeir, Fionchra and the lava-capped summit of Bloodstone Hill are in the island's west.

Rùm is the core of a volcano that developed on a pre-existing structure of Torridonian sandstone and shales resting on Lewisian gneiss. Volcanic activity 65 million years ago formed a dome over a kilometre high and several kilometres across. Pressure from below caused fractures to form around the dome, which collapsed, forming a caldera. The caldera floor was gradually covered by rocks and debris, consisting largely of Torridonian sandstone and Lewisian gneiss, which was compressed, forming rocks known as breccias, found in Coire Dubh. The vestiges of the dome are evident on the slopes of the Rùm Cuillin, where the Torridonian rocks incline steeply away from the adjacent igneous rocks.

Magma, ash and rock erupted into the caldera, along with gas clouds known as pyroclastic flows which formed rocks known as rhyodacites, found around the margins of the Rùm Cuillin and on the ridge between the summits of Ainshval and Sgùrr nan Gillean.

The western hills, including Orval and Àrd Nev, are predominantly composed of coarse-grained granites formed from magma that crystallised below the Earth's surface. The Rùm Cuillin is mostly composed of layers of pale, hard gabbro interspersed with brown, crumbly peridotite, rocks created from cooling magma at the base of the magma chamber, especially on Hallival and Askival. There are some outcrops of the pre-volcanic Lewisian gneiss near Dibidil in the south-east corner of the island, and extensive Torridonian sandstone is found in the north and east.

Basalt dikes are found on the north-west coast between Kilmory and Guirdil: erosion of the less-resistant rock into which the molten magma once flowed has left the dikes exposed as natural walls. They tend to radiate out from a point in Glen Harris, which suggests that this was the centre of volcanic activity. Bloodstone Hill was formed by lava flowing away from this volcanic centre; gas bubbles in the rock filled with heated silica, which cooled to form green agate flecked with red, hence the name 'bloodstone'. The red flecks are tiny crystals of iron minerals, which oxidised on exposure to air.

The last major glaciation of the Quarternary Ice Age began about 30,000 years ago, when glaciers covered the island and the tops of the highest mountains protruded through the ice as 'nunataks'. Frost-shattering created scree slopes on these summits, and freeze-thaw processes have sorted rock particles into remarkable regular patterns such as the stone stripes and polygons near the summit of Orval.

The ice sheets retreated around 10,000BCE. During glacial periods sea levels dropped, rising again when the glaciers melted. The landmass sank under the weight of the ice cap, then rose again as the ice retreated. The land continued to rise beyond the maximum increase in sea level, forming the raised beaches found around the coastline 12–30m above the present sea level, especially between Harris and A' Bhrìdeanach.

With the retreat of the ice sheets, the climate improved; tundra vegetation then gave way to burgeoning forest cover. At its warmest, 6000 years ago, the climate encouraged forestation to a higher altitude than the present day. However, Scotland's climate became cooler and damper around 1000BCE during the Neolithic and early Bronze Age and peat expanded at the expense of woodland. A dearth of cultivable land also led to woodland clearance by early farming communities.

Ruin at Carn-an-dobhrain Bhig, Southside Wood (Walk 11)

HISTORY

Traces from one of the earliest known human settlements in Scotland were found on Rùm at a site near Kinloch. Concentrations of bloodstone microliths indicated the manufacture of stone tools, and roasted hazlenut shells were radiocarbon dated to 6500BCE. A shell midden at Papadil, cave middens at Bagh na h-Uamha and Shellesder, and tidal fish traps at Kinloch and Kilmory are also characteristic of Mesolithic hunter-gatherers.

The Stone Age to St Columba

Peat core samples from Kinloch revealed soil erosion and a decline in tree pollen, suggesting that woodland clearance for cultivation occurred during the Neolithic (New Stone Age), from around 2700BCE. Bronze Age traces on Rùm are limited to hut circle sites and finds of barbed and tanged bloodstone arrow heads.

Iron-working skills and characteristic structures including brochs, duns, wheelhouses, crannogs and souterrains were introduced to Scotland around the middle of the first millennium BCE by Celtic people migrating from continental Europe. Rùm possesses only a few crude promontory fort sites at Kilmory, Papadil and Shellesder. Decorated pottery sherds are the only other Iron Age artefacts retrieved on the island.

The first written references to the early Caledonian people come from the Romans. References to the 'Picti' first appeared in Roman accounts around 300CE, and it is likely that the population of Rùm at this time was Pictish in origin. St Columba came from Ireland around 563 and established a monastery on Iona. Columba's followers, Celtic Christian missionaries, set about converting the populations of the islands and the mainland.

The Viking age
In 794 Iona suffered the first of many Viking raids, which gradually forced the monastery into decline. In common with many Hebridean islands, Rùm came within the Norse sphere of influence. The Norsemen ruled the Small Isles from 833 until the Treaty of Perth in 1266, when the Isle of Man and all the Hebrides were ceded to Scotland.

The Norse legacy is most obvious in the toponymy of the island, whose name may itself derive from the Old Norse *rōm-øy*, meaning 'wide island', or the Gaelic *ì-dhruim*, meaning 'isle of the ridge'. The name 'cuillin' also comes from the Norse *kiolen*, meaning 'high rocks'.

The Middle Ages to the Macleans
During the 13th century the island was in the possession of the powerful Macruari clan for a brief period until 1346, when Rùm was chartered to Clanranald – known as the Lords of the Isles – who ruled much of the Hebrides for 150 years. By the mid-16th century Rùm was in the possession of the Macleans of Coll, then in 1588 the Small Isles were assaulted when Lachlan Maclean of Duart led

The Bullough Mausoleum at Harris Bay (Walks 5 and 9)

Exotic Edwardiana: Kinloch Castle interior

a raiding party including 100 Spanish marines from a galleon of the defeated Armada anchored at Tobermory. The islands' settlements were torched and their inhabitants murdered. By 1593 Clanranald had re-occupied the island, but despite these temporary setbacks the Macleans of Coll kept possession of Rùm for more than three centuries.

By the late 17th century Rùm's population had increased. Conditions were primitive and the dearth of viable farming land stretched resources. The needs of a growing population led to the extermination of the native red deer during the latter half of the 18th century.

At the beginning of the 19th century there were nine hamlets on Rùm and the local economy enjoyed a boost from the kelp industry. However, in 1825 the island was leased to Dr Lachlan Maclean. Like many Highland landlords, Maclean, in search of profit, decided to clear the land and turn it over to 8000 blackface sheep. On 11 July 1826 around 300 inhabitants boarded the *Highland Lad* and the *Dove of Harmony*, bound for Cape Breton in Nova Scotia. The remaining 130 followed in 1828 on the *St Lawrence*. However, mutton and wool prices subsequently declined and the enterprise failed; Lachlan Maclean left Rùm, bankrupt, in 1839.

Into the 20th century

In 1845 Maclean of Coll sold Rùm to the Marquess of Salisbury, who reintroduced red deer and converted the island into a sporting estate. For over a century thereafter, Rùm was known as the 'Forbidden Island', with uninvited visitors actively discouraged. In 1888 Rùm was acquired by John Bullough, a cotton machinery manufacturer from Lancashire. At this time the population numbered between 60 and 70 shepherds, estate workers and their families. When Bullough died in 1891, ownership of the island was assumed by his son, George Bullough.

The most striking legacy of Sir George Bullough – he was knighted in 1901 – is the incongruous and often-maligned Kinloch Castle (Walk 4). Sir George and Lady Monica Bullough usually resided at the castle during the stalking season and would entertain their wealthy and important guests there in some style. Sir George died in France in July 1939 and was interred in the family Mausoleum at Harris Bay. His widow died in 1967, having sold the whole island, save for the Mausoleum, but including the castle and its contents, to the Nature Conservancy Council (NCC) in 1957 for the 'knock-down price of £23,000' on the understanding that it would be used as a National Nature Reserve.

National Nature Reserve (NNR)

The island is still owned and managed as a single estate by the NCC's successors, NatureScot (previously Scottish Natural Heritage). However, in 2010, SNH handed over Kinloch Village to the Isle of Rùm Community Trust to provide land for housing and local enterprises.

In addition to its status as an NNR, Rùm was designated a Biosphere Reserve in 1976, a Site of Special Scientific Interest in 1987, and has 17 sites scheduled as nationally important ancient monuments. In 2024, Rùm was designated Scotland's first International Dark Sky Sanctuary.

The Rùm NNR was originally envisaged as an 'open-air laboratory' with scientific research conducted into specific areas of the island's ecology, most notably the long-term study of the red deer population. Rùm was also the primary site for the ultimately successful reintroduction of the white-tailed eagle to Scotland during the 1970s and 1980s. However, SNH (later NatureScot) shifted the emphasis to recreating a habitat resembling what existed before the island's native tree cover was removed. This has involved the reintroduction of over a million trees and shrubs of 20 native species in the vicinity of Kinloch and Loch Scresort.

WILDLIFE

Rùm's red deer population has been the subject of a long-term study by researchers from Cambridge and Edinburgh universities, based at Kilmory Bay in the north of the island. The research has focussed on the sociobiology and behavioural ecology of red deer. The island's deer population was hunted to extinction in the 18th century, but since reintroduction in 1845 the number has grown to the currently maintained level of around 1500.

Although not actually 'wild' it would be remiss to not include Rùm's small herd of about 14 ponies here. The Rùm ponies are an old breed, and their presence was first recorded in 1772. Shortly thereafter, Dr Johnson described them as 'very small, but of a breed eminent for beauty'. They are of stocky stature, averaging 13 hands in height, with a dark stripe along the back and zebra stripes on the forelegs. These features suggest that they are related to primitive northern European breeds, perhaps introduced by the Norsemen. It is sometimes claimed – erroneously – that they are descended from animals off-loaded from ships of the Spanish Armada. The ponies are used to bring deer carcasses off the hill during the stalking season, but are otherwise left to roam wild.

Rùm's wild goats are subject to the same Armada myth as the ponies, but are in fact descended from domestic animals. The goat stocks were improved for stalking during the Bullough's tenure and were renowned for their impressive horns and thick, shaggy fleeces. The tribe, numbering around 200, usually inhabits the sea cliffs and mountains, particularly in the west. A small fold of around 30 Highland cattle was introduced to the island in 1970.

Atlantic grey and common seals frequent Rùm's coastline, and Eurasian otters patrol territories around the island's shores. Other mammals found on Rùm include the pygmy shrew, pipistrelle bat, brown rat and the island's own strain of long-tailed field mouse, *Apodemus sylvaticus hamiltoni*. The only reptile found on Rùm is the common lizard, and the only amphibian is the palmate newt. There are brown trout, European eels and three-spined sticklebacks in the streams, and occasionally salmon in the Kinloch River.

Rùm is renowned for its 61,000 pairs of Manx shearwaters – one of the world's largest breeding colonies. These migratory birds return to Rùm every summer to breed in underground burrows high in the Cuillin. Trollabhal has high densities of nest burrows, which may have been occupied for many centuries. When the birds swap incubation shifts at night they make a fearsome racket, hence the Norse name for the mountain (Trollabhal means 'Hill of the Trolls'). There are sizeable colonies of fulmars, shags, guillemots, razorbills, kittiwakes and other gulls, mainly found along the south-eastern cliffs.

White-tailed eagles were persecuted to extinction on Rùm by 1912 and became extinct in Scotland thereafter. A programme of reintroduction began on the island in 1975, and within ten years 82 young birds from Norway had been released. Today a successful breeding population is gradually colonising the west coast of Scotland. Several pairs of golden eagles nest on the island; merlin, buzzards, sparrowhawks, peregrines,

Rùm pony mare and foal, Kinloch

kestrels and short-eared owls are the other resident birds of prey. Other bird species include the red-throated diver, red-breasted merganser, eider, shelduck, red grouse, corncrake, oystercatcher, lapwing, golden plover, curlew, cuckoo, raven and hooded crow as well as various finches, tits, chats, thrushes, warblers, pipits and wagtails.

Invertebrates include numerous species of damselfly, dragonfly, beetle, butterfly and moth. Several rare species are found on the slopes of Barkeval, Hallival and Askival, including the ground beetles *Leistus montanus* and *Amara quenseli*. The hugely irritating midge (*Culicoides impunctatus*), a small biting gnat, occurs in unbelievable numbers between mid-spring and mid-autumn. Deer ticks and clegs – an aggressive horse fly – are the island's other bloodthirsty beasties. Ticks can carry Lyme disease, which can become seriously debilitating if undiagnosed and untreated.

WOODLAND, PLANTS AND FLOWERS

By the end of the 18th century much of Rùm's woodland had been cleared for grazing. John Bullough planted 8000 trees at Kilmory, Harris and Kinloch in the 1890s, but only some of those at Kinloch still survive. In 1960 a nursery was established at Kinloch to support the reintroduction of 20 native tree species, including Scots pine, oak, silver birch, aspen, alder, hawthorn, rowan and holly. Over a million native trees and shrubs have since been planted. The forested area is limited to the environs of Kinloch, the slopes surrounding Loch Scresort and on nearby Meall á Ghoirtein.

As a consequence of high rainfall and acid soils 90% of Rùm's vegetation comprises bog and heath. Much of the island is dominated by tussocky purple moor grass and deer sedge. In boggy areas sedges and bog asphodel abound alongside sundew and butterwort. Heather or ling (calluna) occurs in drier areas. The well-fertilised soil beneath the Manx shearwater burrows in the Cuillin keeps the turf green at an unusually high altitude.

Among the island's other flora are the rare arctic sandwort and alpine pennycress, endemic varieties of the heath spotted orchid and eyebright as well as more common species such as blue heath milkwort and roseroot. A total of 590 species of higher plants and ferns have been recorded on Rùm.

GETTING AROUND

Visitors are not permitted to bring vehicles to Rùm but disabled Blue Badge holders should be able to arrange for a vehicle permit if staying overnight. There is no public transport on the island. Getting around on foot is the norm for most visitors, although mountain or gravel bikes can be of use on several of the island's Landrover tracks.

At the time of writing, Rùm Bunkhouse (see below) was in the process of setting up a bike hire service.

AMENITIES

The Isle of Rùm's website (www.isleofrum.com) provides up-to-date listings of amenities and accommodation, as well as other useful information.

All the island's facilities are located in Kinloch or along the shore road between the pier and the village. The small visitor centre, situated along the shore track between the pier and the campsite, is a good introduction to Rùm's natural heritage and some of the walks available. It is usually unstaffed and open all hours – entry is free.

The Isle of Rùm shop (tel 01687 460328) is next to the village hall and stocks bread, fruit and veg, tinned goods, some frozen meat, beers, wines and spirits, as well as serving hot drinks. Groceries can be pre-ordered for large groups with at least a week's notice. The island's post office is at the shop.

There are public toilets at the village hall and also at the campsite. There is a public payphone situated next to the Drift craft shop, which is open daily in summer. Mobile phone coverage is good around Kinloch and the eastern side of the island, but is patchy to non-existent in the west. There is Wi-Fi internet available at the Rùm Bunkhouse (see below) and also at the village hall where a small fee is charged.

The outflow of the Glen Shellesder burn in spate (Walks 5 and 6)

PLACES TO STAY

Aside from the two MBA-maintained bothies at Dibidil and Guirdil (www.mountainbothies.org.uk) and wild camping, all places to stay are found in Kinloch.

The award-winning, community-owned Rùm Bunkhouse (tel 07824 036305 www.rumbunkhouse.com), a couple of pod cabins and the shoreside campsite are maintained by the Isle of Rùm Community Trust. The modern, well-equipped bunkhouse sleeps 20 and has a drying room, a large kitchen, spacious communal areas, a wood-burning stove and large French windows providing panoramic views of Loch Scresort. The cabins sleep up to four people and are supplied with slim mattresses, plugs and USB chargers and a kettle. The beautifully situated campsite has a communal cabin for shelter, storing bags, food etc and has solar USB charging points. It also has a verandah with benches for when the midges aren't biting. The campsite has a standpipe for drinking water, sinks for washing up and a barbecue. Toilets and showers for the cabins and campsite are a short walk away.

The Harbour BBQ Bothy (tel 07906 181029 harbourhut@gmail.com) provides basic accommodation for four to six people in a heptagonal wooden cabin with reindeer-hide rugs, solar lighting and an indoor BBQ grill with chimney.

Situated by the shore of Loch Scresort, Ivy Cottage (tel 01687 462744 www.ivycottageisleofrum.co.uk) has one double and one family room and provides optional vegetarian evening meals and breakfast. Under the same management, the Bramble Bothy shepherd's hut sleeps two and is equipped with a double bed, armchairs, wood burner, fridge, hob and sink, and a composting toilet.

WALK 1
A round of the Rùm Cuillin

Start/finish	Kinloch (NM 402 997)
Time	9–10hr; not including Barkeval 7hr 45min–8hr 45min; to Dibidil bothy 6–7hr
Distance	23.8km (14.8 miles); not including Barkeval 21.4km (23.3 miles); to Dibidil bothy 15.3km (9.5 miles)
Total ascent	2025m (6644ft); not including Barkeval 1903m (6245ft)
Difficulty	This is a long, tough day traversing rugged mountain terrain. The terrain is complex in places and these maritime mountains attract cloud, requiring navigational competence
Terrain	Rugged, rocky mountain terrain. The northernmost hills are formed largely of basalt and gabbro – a coarse-grained rock beloved of climbers and hill walkers for its excellent grip – while the fine-grained felsite capping the southern peaks can be slippery in wet conditions. The walk out on the Dibidil path is boggy in places
Maps	OS Explorer 397; OS Landranger 39; Harvey Maps, Rùm, Eigg, Canna, Muck Superwalker XT25

The Rùm Cuillin are the chain of rocky volcanic mountains that dominate the southern part of Rùm. The northernmost Cuillin are principally formed of peridotite basalt and gabbro, similar in construction to the Black Cuillin of Skye, while the southern peaks are of Torridonian sandstone capped with quartz felsite and Lewisian gneiss. A round of the Rùm Cuillin makes for a magnificent, challenging day in the hills and usually features somewhere on the 'to-do' list of aficionados of the Scottish mountains. A complete round visits the summits of Barkeval (591m), Hallival (722m; 723m according to some maps), Askival (812m), Trollabhal (702m), Ainshval (781m) Sgùrr nan Goibhrean (759m) and Sgùrr nan Gillean (764m).

A round of the Rùm Cuillin is the finest ridge traverse in the Hebrides outside of Skye, although it is nowhere as difficult as Skye's Cuillin Ridge, requiring some moderate scrambling and no climbing other than a couple of short sections that are easily avoided. However, the route does require a substantial physical effort, involving 2025m of ascent and descent; there

WALK 1 – A ROUND OF THE RÙM CUILLIN

are several airy, exposed sections and the weather on Rùm can change very quickly.

It is essential that you have a good level of fitness, good navigation skills and are properly equipped before attempting a round of the Rùm Cuillin. Ensure you have plenty of daylight for completing the route and check weather forecasts before setting out: it is not a walk for very wet, windy conditions or poor visibility.

The round can be walked as a two-day route by incorporating an overnight stop at Dibidil bothy. If this is your plan it is advisable to carry a tent or shelter in case you find the bothy fully occupied.

Approaching **Kinloch Castle** from the direction of the pier, turn left onto a track running along its south side where a marker post with a red plant symbol indicates 'Coire Dubh 2.5km'. Follow the path alongside a burn through woodland. Pass a shed and a generator building where another track joins from the right; keep straight ahead (right) soon passing a National Nature Reserve signpost. Continue following the path alongside the **Allt Slugan a' Choilich** flowing down from Coire Dubh. The woodland becomes sparser before the path emerges onto rising open ground. The path is distinct and easy to follow as it climbs beside the river. Step across a couple of burns flowing into the river along the way and pass a small sluice dam before reaching the **Coire Dubh** at around 270m.

Askival, Ainshval and Trollabhal seen from the summit of Hallival

Ainshval (left) and Trollabhal from the southwest ridge of Askival

Continue along the path next to the Allt Slugan a' Choilich on level ground before arriving at a dilapidated stone dam – where the path marked on the OS Explorer map runs out. Cross the river here: 180m above the corrie to the south-west is the low point of the Bealach Bairc-mheall (466m) between Barkeval and Hallival. Cross the often-wet corrie floor to pick up the rough, intermittent path climbing up to the bealach, which isn't obvious at first, but it keeps to the left of the burn tumbling down into the corrie.

Alternative route avoiding Barkeval
If you're not including Barkeval in your round then follow a distinct path skirting around the eastern side of the corrie. Climb initially south-eastwards to the col at **Cnapan Breaca**, then trend south-south-west, climbing up over a series of wide rocky ledges to gain the foot of Hallival's north-western ridge.

Main route
From the bealach climb north-west to the first cairn (575m) on the summit ridge of **Barkeval** – the actual summit is around 700m west along the ridge. Pass around a couple of weathered basalt outcrops and pick up a vague path to the summit cairn (591m). The superlative views south and south-east onto Hallival, Askival and Trollabhal, towering over the **Atlantic Corrie**, are reason enough to include Barkeval in the traverse. In clear conditions there are fine views south-west down Glen Harris, north-west to the rounded granite hills of Orval, Àrd Nev and Fionchra and north to the Skye Cuillin.

Retrace your route to the bealach, then follow the long ridge, steadily rising south-east to **Hallival**. From below, a band of cliffs runs around the summit, presenting something of an obstacle. However, by keeping to the north-west ridge, where the alternative route rejoins the main route, a way through can be found without difficulty. The summit is marked by a cairn. The views are tremendous, particularly on to Askival's impressive north ridge. Beyond Askival, the summits of Trollabhal, Ainshval, Sgùrr nan Goibhrean and Sgùrr nan Gillean are visible.

From the cairn, continue initially south-west across the summit to begin the 120m descent to the bealach. To avoid steep crags on the south-east face, briefly follow the faint path descending steeply through rocky terrain on the west side of the ridge before trending south-west again to continue down to the bealach. The path climbs a little over a rocky knoll before crossing the bealach and gaining the narrow, grassy north ridge of Askival.

Follow the ridge up towards the steep crags rising to the summit on the north and north-west faces of the mountain. Look out for a path at about 695m before the substantial old cairn is reached and follow the path off the ridge here, skirting around Askival's eastern flank. The path contours and rises gradually at first before climbing more steeply and sinuously through rocky terrain to the summit – its upward progress marked by a number of small cairns. The summit of **Askival** (812m) is marked by a stone-built trig pillar with a low shelter wall. On a clear day the views over to Eigg, Ardnamurchan and Moidart are magnificent.

From the summit, descend along the vague path initially in the lee of the west ridge on its south side. As the path descends it eventually joins the ridge. The terrain is rocky in places, but the 360m descent to the **Bealach an Oir** (455m) presents no problems. The bealach lies at the head of Glen Dibidil and the view south-east along the glen to Eigg and Muck beyond is rather fine. On its north side the bealach drops away into the immense amphitheatre of the Atlantic Corrie, with views over to Barkeval and Hallival. To the south-west, the imposing triumvirate of Ainshval, Sgùrr nan Goibhrean and Sgùrr nan Gillean form the western flank of Glen Dibidil.

From the bealach, climb directly west onto the east ridge of **Trollabhal**, following a reasonably distinct path. The climb is initially straightforward, although a little easy scrambling is required through the craggy terrain encountered between 600m and the mountain's east summit. The slightly higher west summit (702m) is about 50m beyond the east summit and a short, steep descent then ascent via a narrow ridge is required to reach it. There are fine views from the summit along the Harris Buttress and the Triangular Buttress to Harris Bay beyond. To the south, the imposing bulk of Ainshval looms above the Bealach an Fhuarain.

From the east summit the route descends the steep south ridge of Trollabhal to the **Bealach an Fhuarain**. The descent is awkward in places; there is a vague path, but it can be difficult to find its start, especially in poor visibility. Take care to avoid descending into the craggy terrain on the mountain's southern flank. From

WALK 1 – A ROUND OF THE RÙM CUILLIN

the bealach (520m), pass beneath the buttress to the right (west), following a faint path. Continue on the path as it climbs to the right (west) of the buttress rising above the south side of the bealach, then follow tight zigzags up a rocky scree slope before gaining the north-east ridge of **Ainshval** at around 670m. Continue climbing steeply south-south-west in the lee of the north-east ridge, following a fairly distinct path skirting above the Grey Corrie then trending south-eastwards before eventually arriving at the cairn-marked summit (781m).

From the cairn, follow the path south along the whale-backed summit ridge, gradually descending around 100m to a narrow bealach before making the short ascent of **Sgùrr nan Goibhrean** (759m). From the summit, descend a short way before continuing south-east along the ridge, gaining just a little height to arrive at the summit of **Sgùrr nan Gillean** (764m), which is marked with a cairn. The east ridge of Sgùrr nan Gillean drops into an area of steep crags, so the descent should be made initially via the south ridge for 300m before swinging east in a traversing descent, which is boggy and tussocky in places, to **Glen Dibidil** and **Dibidil bothy**. Built in 1849, Dibidil bothy was a ruined shepherd's cottage renovated by a Mountain Bothies Association work party in 1970 (see Walk 5).

To return to Kinloch, cross the **Dibidil River** with care and follow the pony path for 8.5km back to the track road running between the pier and the castle. The path is generally distinct, but be careful not to lose it. There are several burns to cross en route, which can be hazardous during wet weather. On reaching the track road, turn left for **Kinloch** and the castle, turn right for the pier.

Sgùrr nan Gillean (left) rising above the Dibidil River

WALK 2
The Dibidil Horseshoe

Start/finish	Dibidil bothy (NM 393 927)
Alternative start/finish	Kinloch (NM 402 997)
Time	5–6hr; the walk in/out from Kinloch adds 3–3hr 30min each way
Distance	10.5km (6.5 miles); the walk in/out from Kinloch adds 8.5km (5.3 miles) each way
Total ascent	1530m (5020ft); from Kinloch 2195m (7200ft)
Difficulty	This is a fairly tough day's hillwalking in rugged terrain Navigational competence is required as the terrain is complex in places and these maritime mountains attract cloud
Terrain	Rugged, rocky mountain terrain
Maps	OS Explorer 397; OS Landranger 39; Harvey Maps, Rùm, Eigg, Canna, Muck Superwalker XT25
Note	The route from Kinloch to Dibidil is described in detail in Walk 5, Day 1. The return from Dibidil to Kinloch is described in Walk 1

The spectacularly located Dibidil bothy provides the ideal base from which to traverse the horseshoe of peaks flanking wild and rugged Glen Dibidil – Beinn nan Stac, Askival, Trollabhal, Ainshval, Sgùrr nan Goibhrean and Sgùrr nan Gillean. The horseshoe can be traversed in either direction, although the lesser ascent of Beinn nan Stac (546m) offers an easier start than the steep south-eastern flank of Sgùrr nan Gillean (764m). There are several opportunities for scrambling on this route, including the south ridge of Askival, which is more difficult than anything encountered on the Rùm Cuillin traverse, though this can be avoided. The Dibidil Horseshoe is a magnificent route with some outstanding mountain scenery and spectacular views over the neighbouring islands and mainland mountains. The horseshoe traverse can be combined with an overnight stop at Dibidil bothy either before or after the walk (or both!) before returning to Kinloch.

From **Dibidil bothy** head towards Kinloch on the pony path, recrossing the **Dibidil River** before climbing to around 100m along the flank of **Beinn nan Stac**. Leave the path at NM 400 930 by Cnoc nan Cuilèan to climb north along the mountain's south ridge. Just below the summit of Beinn nan Stac there is a short scramble through a line of crags – this can be avoided by continuing north-west to the broad col between Beinn nan Stac and Askival. To the north-west, Clough's Crag rises up in two tiers towards the Askival Prow below the east ridge

From the col, continue climbing north along the south ridge of **Askival** directly towards the summit. This route makes for moderate to difficult scrambling on good rock for around 250m height over the course of several hundred metres distance. This scramble can be avoided by traversing to the south-west of the summit, through rocky terrain, and gaining the west ridge where a vague path can be followed to the summit. The summit (812m) is marked by a stone-built OS trig pillar with a low shelter wall. On a clear day the views across Rùm and over the surrounding islands and west coast mountains are magnificent.

Aiming for the **Bealach an Oir**, descend back along the vague path in the lee of the west ridge on its south side until it joins the west ridge. You should reach the bealach (455m) without difficulties.

The **Bealach an Oir** lies at the head of Glen Dibidil and the view south-east along the glen to Eigg and Muck beyond is rather fine. On its north side the bealach drops away into the immense amphitheatre of the Atlantic Corrie, with views over to Barkeval and Hallival. To the south-west, the imposing triumvirate of Ainshval, Sgùrr nan Goibhrean and Sgùrr nan Gillean form the western flank of Glen Dibidil.

Scrambling on Askival's rocky south ridge

WALK 2 – THE DIBIDIL HORSESHOE

From the bealach, climb directly west onto the east ridge of **Trollabhal**, following a reasonably distinct path. The climb is initially straightforward, although a little easy scrambling is required through the craggy terrain encountered between 600m and the mountain's east summit. The slightly higher west summit (702m) is about 50m beyond the east summit and a short, steep descent then ascent via a narrow ridge is required to reach it. There are fine views from the summit along the Harris Buttress and the Triangular Buttress to Harris Bay beyond. To the south, the imposing bulk of Ainshval looms above the Bealach an Fhuarain.

Wispy cloud on Trollabhal's summit

From the east summit the route descends the steep south ridge of Trollabhal to the **Bealach an Fhuarain**. The descent is awkward in places; there is a vague path, but it can be difficult to find its start, especially in poor visibility. Take care to avoid descending into the craggy terrain on the mountain's southern flank. From the bealach (520m), pass beneath the buttress to the west, following a faint path. Continue on the path as it climbs to the right (west) of the buttress rising above the south side of the bealach, then crosses a rocky scree slope before gaining the north-east ridge of Ainshval around 670m. Continue climbing steeply south-west in the lee of the north-east ridge, following a fairly distinct path skirting above the Grey Corrie before eventually arriving at the cairn-marked summit of **Ainshval** (781m).

From the cairn, follow the path south along the whale-backed summit ridge, gradually descending around 100m to a narrow bealach before making the short ascent of **Sgùrr nan Goibhrean** (759m). From the summit, descend a short way before continuing south-east along the ridge, gaining just a little height to arrive at the summit of **Sgùrr nan Gillean** (764m), which is marked with a cairn. The east ridge of Sgùrr nan Gillean drops into an area of steep crags, so the descent should be made initially via the south ridge for 300m before swinging east in a traversing descent, which is boggy and tussocky in places, to **Glen Dibidil** and **Dibidil bothy**.

WALK 3
Askival and Hallival from Kinloch

Start/finish	Kinloch (NM 402 997)
Time	5–6hr
Distance	11.8km (7.3 miles)
Total ascent	1010m (3315ft)
Difficulty	A robust day's hillwalking taking in the Rùm Cuillin's two highest summits, involving just over 1000m of ascent. These maritime mountains attract cloud, therefore navigational competence is essential
Terrain	Rugged, rocky mountain terrain
Maps	OS Explorer 397; OS Landranger 39; Harvey Maps, Rùm, Eigg, Canna, Muck Superwalker XT25

Vikings sailing through the Sound of Rùm more than a thousand years ago named the island's highest summit Askival – 'the spear-shaped mountain'. Seen from the ferry approaching the Isle of Rùm across the sound today, it's easy to follow their thinking. Indeed, the entire horseshoe of black, volcanic peaks framing sea-facing Glen Dibidil is both impressive and a little intimidating.

The quickest and most straightforward way to climb Askival is from Kinloch via the Bealach Bairc-mheall and Hallival, the neighbouring summit to the north. The walk into the Coire Dubh from Kinloch is relatively short, soon delivering you into the rugged realm of the Rùm Cuillin. This is an exhilarating walk further enlivened by a little easy scrambling, with some tremendous views across Rùm's hinterland to the islands and mainland mountains beyond. However, the ridges and summits are exposed to the elements and island weather can change rapidly, so check forecasts before setting out.

Approaching **Kinloch Castle** from the direction of the pier, turn left onto a track running along its south side where a marker post with a red plant symbol indicates 'Coire Dubh 2.5km'. Follow the path alongside a burn through woodland. Pass a shed and a generator building where another track joins from the right; keep straight ahead (right) soon passing a National Nature Reserve signpost.

WALK 3 – ASKIVAL AND HALLIVAL FROM KINLOCH

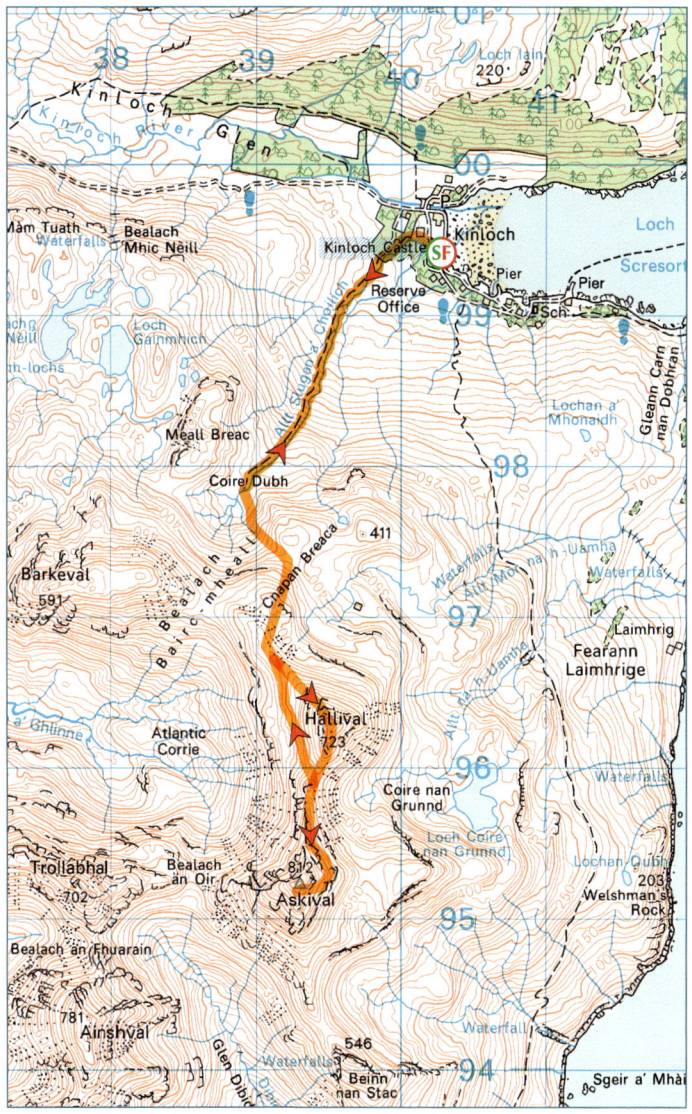

On the north ridge beneath the Askival Pinnacle

Continue following the path alongside the **Allt Slugan a' Choilich** flowing down from Coire Dubh. The woodland becomes sparser before the path emerges onto rising open ground. The path is distinct and easy to follow as it climbs beside the river. Step across a couple of burns flowing into the river along the way and pass a sculptural metal sundial.

> The **sundial**, with text describing 'A Year in the Life of a Manx Shearwater', serves as a memorial to Wilf Nelson who was Rùm's nature reserve warden between 1987 and 1989. He tragically fell to his death from Bloodstone Hill in September 1989 while carrying out wildlife observations.

Continue past a small sluice dam before reaching the lip of the **Coire Dubh** at around 270m.

Continue along the path next to the Allt Slugan a' Choilich on level ground before arriving at a dilapidated stone dam – where the path marked on the OS Explorer map runs out. Cross the river here: 180m above the corrie to the south-west, is the low point of the **Bealach Bairc-mheall** (466m) between Barkeval and Hallival. However, unless you're also including Barkeval in your itinerary, follow the path skirting around the eastern side of the corrie. Climb initially south-eastwards to the col at **Cnapan Breaca**, then trend south-south-west, climbing up over a series of wide rocky ledges to gain the foot of Hallival's north-western ridge.

Follow the long ridge, steadily rising south-east to **Hallival**. From below, a band of cliffs runs around the summit, presenting something of an obstacle. However, a route through these cliffs can be found without difficulty by keeping to the north-west ridge. The summit is marked by a cairn and the views are tremendous, particularly on to Askival's impressive north ridge. Beyond Askival, the summits of Trollabhal, Ainshval, Sgùrr nan Goibhrean and Sgùrr nan Gillean are visible.

From the cairn, continue initially south-west across the summit to begin the 120m descent to the bealach. To avoid steep crags on the south-east face, descend steeply following the faint path through rocky terrain on the west side of the ridge briefly before trending south-west again to continue down to the bealach. The path climbs a little over a rocky knoll before crossing the bealach and gaining the narrow, grassy north ridge of **Askival**.

Follow the ridge up towards the steep crags rising to the summit on the north and north-west faces of the mountain, look for a substantial old cairn at around 695m and follow the path off the ridge here, skirting around Askival's eastern flank. The path contours and rises gradually at first before climbing more steeply and sinuously through rocky terrain to the summit – its upward progress marked by a number of small cairns. Numerous Manx shearwater nest burrows perforate the grassy slopes between the rock tiers on the mountain's flanks. The summit is marked by a stone-built trig pillar with a low shelter wall. On a clear day the views over to Eigg, Ardnamurchan and Moidart are magnificent.

Alternatively, for competent scramblers the higher reaches of the north ridge provide some quality entertainment. Blocky, broken rock leads up towards the Askival Pinnacle, which is more of a step in the ridge than a true pinnacle and makes for a brief though exposed moderate scramble if taken directly. More robust clambering along the crest follows before the summit is gained.

Return to the bealach from where you can contour along the western flank of **Hallival** above the Atlantic Corrie, unless you feel it needs climbing a second time! Regain Hallival's north-west ridge above the **Bealach Bairc-mheall** and retrace the outward route via the **Cnapan Breaca** and **Coire Dubh** back to **Kinloch**.

WALK 4
Hallival and Barkeval from Kinloch

Start/finish	Kinloch (NM 402 997)
Time	4–5hr; excluding Barkeval 3hr 30min–4hr; excluding Hallival 3hr–3hr 30min
Distance	11.3km (7 miles); excluding Barkeval 9.3km (5.8 miles); excluding Hallival 8.9km (5.5 miles)
Total ascent	825m (2705ft); excluding Barkeval 715m (2345ft); excluding Hallival 576m (1890ft)
Difficulty	Although these are the most easily accessible of the Rùm Cuillin's summits, they should not be underestimated. This route involves substantial ascent on rugged terrain. On the hill, paths are indistinct and navigational competence is essential in case of poor visibility
Terrain	Rugged, rocky mountain terrain
Maps	OS Explorer 397; OS Landranger 39; Harvey Maps, Rùm, Eigg, Canna, Muck Superwalker XT25

The most northerly peaks of the Rùm Cuillin, Hallival (722m; 723m according to some maps) and Barkeval (591m) are the nearest to Kinloch and arguably the easiest to climb, making them the most accessible summits along the entire ridge. Certainly, climbing either or both of Hallival and Barkeval makes for the shortest available hillwalking option from Rùm's only settlement.

From Kinloch, the walk up along the Allt Slugan a' Choillich into the Coire Dubh, cradled beneath the northern flank of the ridge, is relatively short and the rugged spine of the Rùm Cuillin is gained soon after. This stimulating walk is further enhanced by a little very easy scrambling through rock bands near Hallival's summit. Both summits enjoy some tremendous views of Askival and the other Cuillin summits as well as across Rùm's hinterland to the islands and mainland mountains beyond. However, island weather can change quickly, so check forecasts before setting out to avoid poor visibility and adverse conditions on these exposed hills.

WALK 4 – HALLIVAL AND BARKEVAL FROM KINLOCH

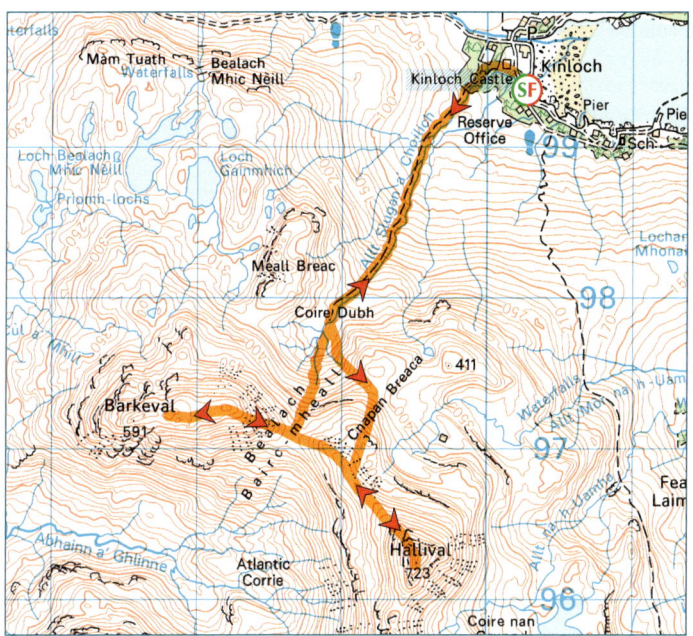

Approaching **Kinloch Castle** from the direction of the pier, turn left onto a track running along its south side where a marker post with a red plant symbol indicates 'Coire Dubh 2.5km'. Follow the path alongside a burn through woodland. Pass a shed and a generator building where another track joins from the right; keep straight ahead (right) soon passing a National Nature Reserve signpost. Continue following the path alongside the **Allt Slugan a' Choilich** flowing down from Coire Dubh. The woodland becomes sparser before the path emerges onto rising open ground. The path is distinct and easy to follow as it climbs beside the river. Step across a couple of burns flowing into the river along the way and pass a sculptural metal sundial (see Walk 3). Continue past a small sluice dam before reaching the lip of the **Coire Dubh** at around 270m.

Continue along the path next to the Allt Slugan a' Choilich on level ground before arriving at a dilapidated stone dam – where the path marked on the OS Explorer map runs out. Cross the river here: 180m above the corrie to the south-west, is the low point of the **Bealach Bairc-mheall** (466m) between Barkeval and Hallival.

Route excluding Hallival
If you're climbing only Barkeval head directly across the often-wet corrie floor making for the foot of the burn flowing down from the bealach. Pick up the intermittent rough path climbing along the left-hand side of the burn to reach the bealach. Now go to 'Main route including Barkeval' (below).

Main route including Hallival
Follow the path from the corrie floor skirting around the eastern side of the corrie and climb initially south-eastwards to the col at **Cnapan Breaca**, then trend south-south-west, climbing up over a series of wide rocky ledges to gain the foot of Hallival's north-western ridge. Follow the long ridge, steadily rising south-east to **Hallival**. From below, a band of cliffs runs around the summit, presenting something of an obstacle. However, a route through these cliffs can be found without difficulty by keeping to the north-west ridge. The summit is marked by a cairn and the views are tremendous, particularly on to Askival's impressive north ridge. Beyond Askival, the summits of Trollabhal, Ainshval, Sgùrr nan Goibhrean and Sgùrr nan Gillean are visible.

Route excluding Barkeval
Retrace your outward route to return to **Kinloch**.

Main route including Barkeval
Follow Hallival's north-western ridge all the way down to the **Bealach Bairc-mheall** (466m). Those climbing only Barkeval rejoin the main route at the bealach. From the bealach climb steadily north-westwards to the first cairn (575m) on the summit ridge of **Barkeval** – the actual summit is around 700m west along the ridge, which broadens and levels out beyond the cairn. Pass a couple of weathered basalt outcrops and pick up a vague path on the south side of the ridge before bearing right to the summit cairn (591m).

> The superlative **views** south and south-east onto Hallival, Askival and Trollabhal, towering over the Atlantic Corrie, are reason enough to include Barkeval in your itinerary. In clear conditions there are fine views south-west down Glen Harris, north-west to the rounded granite hills of Orval, Àrd Nev and Fionchra and north to the Skye Cuillin.

Retrace your route to the **Bealach Bairc-mheall** then descend north north-eastwards following the path running down along the right-hand side of the burn flowing into the **Coire Dubh** below. Cross the burn by the dilapidated dam and follow your outward route back to **Kinloch**.

Kinloch Castle

KINLOCH CASTLE

The most striking legacy of Sir George Bullough is the incongruous and often-maligned Kinloch Castle, built from red sandstone during the last years of the 19th century and completed in 1902. A hundred stonemasons and craftsmen were brought from Lancashire, and Sir George purportedly paid the workforce extra to wear kilts of Rùm plaid.

The estate employed around 100 people, including 14 under-gardeners to maintain the extensive grounds, which included a nine-hole golf course, a bowling green, tennis and racquets courts, heated ornamental turtle and alligator ponds and an aviary housing birds of paradise and hummingbirds. Soil for the grounds was imported from Ayrshire, and grapes, peaches, nectarines and figs were grown in the estate's glasshouses.

The interior boasted an orchestrion – a mechanical contrivance that simulated the sounds of brass, drum and woodwind – an air-conditioned billiards room and an ingenious and elaborate central-heating system, which fed piping hot water to the Heath Robinson-esque bathrooms, replete with 'jacuzzi', while also heating the glasshouses and ornamental ponds.

The estate fell into disrepair during and after the First World War. For some years the castle functioned as a hostel. However, the hostel was closed in 2015 and the castle's long-term future remains uncertain. At the time of this book's publication, Kinloch Castle remains closed to the public.

Heading up along the Allt Slugan a' Choilich to the Coire Dubh (Walk 4)

WALK 5
Around the coast of Rùm

Heading north-west from Guirdil with Bloodstone Hill behind (Day 3)

Start	Dibidil pony path, between Loch Scresort ferry slipway and Kinloch Castle (NM 404 991)
Finish	Kinloch (NM 402 997)
Time	3 days
Distance	41.6km (25.8 miles); via Kilmory and Kinloch glens 39.1km (24.3 miles)
Total ascent	2000m (6562ft); via Kilmory and Kinloch glens 1795m (5889ft)
Difficulty	The rough, uneven terrain is especially demanding with a heavy backpack. Mostly pathless beyond Papadil. Good navigation skills needed despite this being a largely coastal route
Terrain	The terrain is at times rough, boggy and tussocky, but nowhere unmanageable. The generally good path between Kinloch and Papadil can be vague in places and very wet after heavy rain. The easier option return to Kinloch from Kilmory follows a metalled track
Maps	OS Explorer 397; OS Landranger 39; Harvey Maps, Rùm, Eigg, Canna, Muck Superwalker XT25

WALK 5 – AROUND THE COAST OF RÙM

Although the Rùm Cuillin provide the focus for many visiting walkers, the island also boasts a wild coastline that is at times spectacular with rugged cliffs, rocky shores, magnificent white-sand bays and remarkable geological features. Furthermore, traversing Rùm's coastline gives superlative views of the surrounding islands and the mainland mountains and coastline. A complete circumambulation of the coastline of Rùm only amounts to around 40km, but three days is a sensible time to allow as the nature of the terrain makes progress slower and more physically demanding than walking on established footpaths,

Hallival seen from Coire nan Gruund (Day 1)

particularly when carrying camping gear and food. At the end of the 19th century, a guest of George Bullough's, by the name of Harry Hinton, won a bet that he could run round the island within 4hr! This seems a wildly implausible feat.

The Mountain Bothies Association (MBA)-maintained bothies at Dibidil and Guirdil make for obvious overnight stops along this route, but it is advisable to carry a tent or shelter in case you find them fully occupied. Driftwood is scarce – at Dibidil in particular – so it's worth carrying in some kindling and coal if you can. Bothies are simple shelters for all hill-goers to use – please do so responsibly. You can join the Mountain Bothies Association at www.mountainbothies.org.uk.

The section of coastline between Kinloch and Papadil benefits from an old pony path and thereafter stretches of faint path – often deer and goat tracks – aid progress through the wild terrain. The route traverses terrain that is at times boggy and tussocky or with dense heather-cover, but it is nowhere unmanageable except in the very north-east of the island, which this route bypasses in any case.

Drinking water can be collected from the burns which run off the hills at frequent intervals – be sure to collect your water where the stream is visibly moving. You are responsible for carrying your own rubbish out with you. Human waste should always be buried well away from bothies and water sources.

The path between Kinloch and Dibidil can rapidly become impassable when burns are in spate after heavy rain. Do not attempt to cross rivers in spate – if you are swept away your chances of survival are very small. If you manage to cross one river in these conditions you may come up against an impassable torrent further on; if you then attempt to recross the river you previously crossed, you may find that it is running higher and faster than before.

DAY 1
Kinloch to Dibidil

Start	Dibidil pony path, between Loch Scresort ferry slipway and Kinloch Castle (NM 404 991)
Finish	Dibidil bothy (NM 393 927)
Time	3–3hr 30min
Distance	8.5km (5.3 miles)
Ascent	385m (1265ft)
Difficulty	A short day, but with a significant amount of climbing. Not to be underestimated with a heavy rucksack. There are four burns to cross that are potentially dangerous in spate
Terrain	Rough, often boggy moorland that does, however, benefit from a good path for much of the way

The bothy at Dibidil is only a 3–3hr 30min walk from Kinloch. Other options are to continue to Papadil (4hr 30min–5hr 30min) or Harris Bay (7–8hr 30min) and bivouac at either of these wonderful spots.

From the ferry slipway, follow the track road to a junction where a signpost indicates the old stone slipway to the right and the castle and other amenities straight ahead. Take neither, but keep to the left-hand track road for a further 400m then turn left just before a set of white-painted gates where the Dibidil pony path begins its gradual climb south. (A wooden marker post indicates that Dibidil is 8.5km distant.) If starting from **Kinloch Castle** head south-east along the track/road, keeping straight ahead at the path junction: pass through the white-painted gates and join the Dibidil path to your right shortly after.

The path climbs steadily to 200m and, as Loch Scresort drops away behind you, the pyramidal summit of Hallival comes in to view to the south-west and mighty Askival soon emerges from its lee.

The **Dibidil path** actually extends as far as Papadil and was built as a pony path in the mid-19th century at the direction of the Marquess of Salisbury, then owner of Rùm. It is metalled in places with large stones and some sections have been improved with drainage culverts and gravel. However, there are also some

Walk 5 – Around the coast of Rùm

Leaving Kinloch behind on the Dibidil path

potentially very boggy sections. Other than the signpost at the beginning there are no waymarkers so it is worth paying attention to the path as it can be easy to lose it in places – especially if distracted by the fantastic views.

The path contours along, gaining and losing a little height. After 2km the **Allt Mòr na h-Uamha** burn is crossed followed by the **Allt na h-Uamha** – crossing can be tricky if the burn is in spate. Choose your crossing point carefully.

Continue contouring along, with Hallival and Askival looming over the Coire nan Grunnd above the path to the west. The huge boulders scattered in the corrie were deposited by a glacier, which once flowed from Hallival. As the path passes above **Lochan Dubh**, the view south-east to Eigg opens up magnificently – soon the entire island lies before you like a huge basalt comma – and shortly after, the tiny isle of Muck also appears. The path, bolstered with gravel and stone steps, drops to 100m in a broad zigzag to cross the Allt nam Bà by way of a ford across a rock slab. If the burn is in spate, cross via some stones nearer to the rock pool beneath the narrow fissure in the rock.

Continue around the flank of **Beinn nan Stac** on the 100m contour. Eventually the view opens up across to Sgùrr nan Gileann, Sgùrr nan Goibhrean and Ainshval towering above the western side of Glen Dibidil. The path descends into **Glen Dibidil** and the bothy soon comes into view. Follow the path

WALK 5 – AROUND THE COAST OF RÙM

Dibidil bothy with Beinn nan Stac (right) and Askival

down to cross the **Dibidil River** at a ford, although you may have to cross higher upstream when the river is in spate – do so with caution. Beyond the river you will come to **Dibidil bothy**.

DIBIDIL BOTHY

Built in 1849, Dibidil bothy was a ruined shepherd's cottage, which was renovated by a work party from the Mountain Bothies Association (MBA) in 1970. The story of the Dibidil bothy renovation is recounted in the late Irvine Butterfield's book, *Dibidil: A Hebridean Adventure*, which was first published in 1972 and was reprinted by the MBA in 2010, the year after Mr. Butterfield's death.

The bothy has two large rooms, one with a hearth, the other with a woodburning stove. However, there is little driftwood to be gleaned from the shore here, so you may want to bring some kindling and coal or peat briquettes with you. One room has a wide two-tier sleeping platform. Beware of deep fissures in the terrain to the south of the bothy.

From the bothy the views up Glen Dibidil are magnificent. Directly across the Sound of Rùm, Eigg lies resplendent and lights from the scattered settlement of Cleadale twinkle across the water after dusk.

DAY 2
Dibidil to Guirdil

Start	Dibidil bothy (NM 393 927)
Finish	Guirdil bothy (NG 319 013)
Time	7hr 30min–9hr
Distance	17.3km (10.7 miles)
Ascent	975m (3200ft)
Difficulty	Mostly continuous path as far as Papadil; rough pathless terrain between Papadil and Guirdil excepting Harris Bay. Route-finding requires diligence. This is a long, tough day with a heavy backpack
Terrain	Rough, and intermittently boggy moorland and rugged coastal walking

This is the longest, toughest day of the route. There are a number of river crossings, high cliffs to traverse and a steep descent into Glen Guirdil. Much of the route is pathless and it is exposed during rough weather. The considerable upside comes in the wonderful coastal landscapes traversed and the tremendous views en route.

Climb to the rear of the bothy to regain the pony path. Most of the way to Papadil the path is quite distinct, although it is vague in places and can be easy to lose in the complex and boggy terrain. The path climbs steadily to 200m then contours along, passing the southern tip of **Loch Dubh an Sgòir**, where it is a little indistinct. The path soon begins a gradual descent as **Loch Papadil** emerges below to the north-west. The path can be easy to lose as it zigzags down to the loch.

If you plan to camp at Papadil, turn left to skirt around the south-east shore of the loch and cross the outflow to find the best bivouac spots near the beach or above the south-west shore of the loch.

Otherwise make for the south-west corner of the small woodland: look out for a rusting iron gate and enter the woodland next to it rather than attempting to pass around the edge of the loch. Pass through the woodland, which can be difficult going – boggy with some dense rhododendron growth; cross a burn and look out for the eerie, roofless ruins of **Papadil Lodge**.

WALK 5 – AROUND THE COAST OF RÙM

Papadil Lodge was built as a shooting lodge by John Bullough, shortly after he took possession of the island in 1888. Shooting parties would be ferried around to the lodge in the estate boat, the servants having already made the journey over from Kinloch by pony.

From Papadil Lodge, cross a burn and exit the woods. The path runs out here and the landscape ahead is formidable prospect, with the flanks of Leac a' Chaisteil and Ruinsival tumbling precipitously down to the wild and rocky shore. Cross another burn at the head of the loch and make for an iron gate, noting the view of the Papadil Pinnacle – a jutting finger of rock standing by the shore at the southern end of the loch. Go through the gate – there is no fence – then pass through a second gate and climb steadily north-east, working your way up to 120m before contouring along. Continue into the broad gully of the Allt na Gile, contour around and cross the burn. Gain a little height and contour along at around 150m through rocky terrain.

Walk 5 – Around the coast of Rùm

Loch Papadil

Gradually gain height over the next kilometre, climbing to 250m – look out for a large cairn where the flank of Ruinsival is turned. This marks the start of a path that contours around the flank of **Ruinsival** before gradually descending.

The **view** opens up along to Harris Bay and the dramatic coastline beyond, including the prow of A' Bhrìdeanach at Rùm's western extremity, with Canna beyond. When free of cloud, the smooth summits of Àrd Nev and Orval rise to the west of Glen Harris.

Follow the path down to cross the **Abhainn Fiachanais** – find a safe crossing point, otherwise follow the river upstream towards the outflow of Loch Fiachanais until you do. The path continues north-west, soon crossing the **Abhainn Rangail** on a substantial wooden bridge. Continue on the track, skirting an impressive raised beach and keeping to the right of some cairns; if the rivers are in spate, continue along the track to cross the Glen Duian River via the bridge, then follow the track to the remarkable **Bullough Mausoleum**. Otherwise, on passing some drystone-walled enclosures head diagonally (south-west) towards the shore – there is an excellent bivouac site in a rectangular enclosure above the beach. Cross the outflow of the **Glen Duian River** and climb a short way to the mausoleum – an unlikely Grecian temple perched upon the wild Hebridean shore. There

BULLOUGH MAUSOLEUM

When John Bullough died in 1891, his remains were interred in an even more ostentatious mausoleum than the present one. The original was cut into the rock at the north-western extremity of Harris Bay and included an octagonal stone tower and interior decorated with Italian mosaic tiles. Allegedly, a tactless guest of Sir George Bullough observed that the Mausoleum was redolent of a public lavatory at Waterloo Station. Sir George had his father's sandstone sarcophagus removed and promptly dynamited the offending structure. John Bullough's remains were finally interred nearby in the neo-classical edifice still standing today, where Sir George and Lady Monica would eventually join him.

is a great level, grassy bivouac site down by the shore on the opposite side of the Glen Duian River from the Bullough Mausoleum.

The section between Harris Bay and Guirdil should take 3hr 30min–4hr 30min. From the mausoleum, follow the drystone wall as it climbs away from the bay. In clear conditions there are spectacular views west to the Rùm Cuillin. Once beyond the wall continue north-west, making for the rocky summit of **Gualann na Pairce**. Pass between the twin, rock-scattered peaks (228m and 232m) and continue north-west, soon losing a little height. Pass to the left of a small **lochan** and

Ruinsival, Harris Bay and the Bullough Mausoleum

WALK 5 – AROUND THE COAST OF RÙM

Guirdil bothy and Bloodstone Hill

cross an area of boggy, hummocky open ground. Steer a course inland from the cliff edge. Pass to the right of another small **lochan** close to the cliff edge. Cross a couple of burns, gain a little height and look out for a faint path, which makes the going much easier through the dense heather cover.

The path runs closer to the clifftops, passing near the cliff edge as it reaches the 250m contour. It is more distinct by this point and it's worth staying with it as it climbs to 300m above **Sgorr Reidh**, with views across to the steep, grassy slope sliding down to Wreck Bay. On a clear day, the views from here along to A' Bhrìdeanach, with Canna, Barra and South Uist beyond, are spectacular. From Sgorr Reidh the clifftop path runs too close to a very big drop, so climb up towards a large cairn at around 300m, then contour around the flank of **Sròn an t-Saighdeir**, trending north then north-east, following deer paths where you can. Lose some height and pass by the south-east end of spectacle-shaped Spectacle Lochan, continuing north-east towards **Bealach an Dubh-bhraigh**, between Sròn an t-Saighdeir and Bloodstone Hill. Cross the open ground of the bealach and pass a small lochan as the view on to Glen Guirdil opens up, with Fionchra to the north-east and the towering cliffs of Orval looming above the head of the glen to the east.

From here, head north-west, along the north-east flank of **Bloodstone Hill**, losing only a little height initially. There are vague traces of path here, which stay above areas of scree on the steep slope. Keep contouring at around 240m for

GUIRDIL BOTHY

Guirdil bothy is a former shepherd's cottage, built in 1848 and renovated by the MBA. It is a fine bothy in a remarkable location, perched above the shore at the mouth of Glen Guirdil beneath the steep flanks of Bloodstone Hill and with fine views across the sound to Sanday and Canna. Guirdil Bay is the site of a former crofting settlement, but the discovery of prehistoric burial cairns here indicates much earlier human occupation. These early settlers were attracted to the site by a seam of bloodstone, a crystalline green agate flecked with red spots of oxidised jasper, which gives Creag nan Stardean – the lava-capped hill towering above Guirdil – its common name.

Bloodstone could be worked to make tools including knives and scrapers as well as arrowheads. Examples of such artefacts originating on Rùm have been found far and wide throughout the Hebrides. Fragments still break off from the seam on the face of Bloodstone Hill and can be picked up on the slopes and the beach below the summit.

A kilometre north-east of Guirdil bothy, beneath the cliffs where the Glen Shellesder burn cascades to the shore by way of a fine waterfall, there is a remarkable stretch of coastline full of impressive geological features including subterranean tunnels, cavernous caves and a huge rock arch. This area is really worth exploring from Guirdil bothy and is also the most likely source of driftwood in the vicinity.

600m or so, then descend steadily along a path to cross two burns descending gullies at obvious points around 140m. Once over, descend very steeply on a grassy slope heading for the south-east corner of a deer-fenced plantation. Once down, continue along the east side of the plantation, then follow the track above the **Guirdil River** down to the beach, crossing the outflow wherever is easiest to arrive at **Guirdil bothy**.

DAY 3
Guirdil to Kinloch

Start	Guirdil bothy (NG 319 013)
Finish	Kinloch
Time	5hr 30min–6hr 30min; via Kilmory and Kinloch glens 5–6hr
Distance	15.8km (9.8 miles); via Kilmory, Kinloch glens 13.3km (8.3 miles)
Ascent	640m (2100ft); via Kilmory and Kinloch glens 435m (1425ft)
Difficulty	Moderately rough going for the greater part. Following the route over Mullach Mòr requires navigational competence
Terrain	Rough, mostly pathless moorland, hill and coastal terrain. Good, metalled track if following the Kilmory and Kinloch glens route

This day's walk starts along a good path to Glen Shellesder, then fainter traces as far as Kilmory, where the island's red deer research HQ is based. It is worth exploring the few kilometres of wonderful coastline beyond Kilmory Bay but there is little to gain from attempting to walk around to Kinloch along the final north-eastern stretch of coastline: a few kilometres east of Kilmory the coastal terrain becomes very boggy, tussocky and difficult to negotiate, and beyond the beach at Samhnan Insir the fine scenery recedes. Instead, there are two options: continue over Mullach Mòr (304m) from Samhnan Insir to Kinloch – this route is best suited in clear conditions as the terrain is complex and can be rough in places; alternatively, turn around, return to Kilmory Bay to follow the Land Rover track up along Kilmory Glen then down Kinloch Glen to Kinloch.

From the **Guirdil bothy**, follow the initially vague path zigzagging east on to the clifftops then winding its way for 1km to **Glen Shellesder**. The path leads to a ford which crosses the **Glen Shellesder burn**, but this can be deep and fast moving after wet weather. There are potentially easier crossing points around 100m upstream near a sharp bend to the left, but beware slippery rocks. Alternatively,

WALKING RÙM AND THE SMALL ISLES

WALK 5 – AROUND THE COAST OF RÙM

Kilmory Bay

if the tide is sufficiently low it is possible to descend the stepped grassy slopes alongside the waterfall where the burn flows out to the sea and cross the burn as near to the shore as possible across the shingle bank, but not across the sand as this is cut by a deep channel. Once across, climb the slopes to regain the clifftop.

The path soon turns east to continue up through Glen Shellesder parallel to the burn, but leave it here, climbing away from the burn and continuing north-east across country, gaining some height. Follow deer paths where possible, as the terrain is boggy in places. Make for a weathered pillow lava outcrop atop a rise, descend a little across open ground then climb a little again, making for a rocky spur. Skirt around this then descend to follow an obvious deer path across an area of boggy open ground.

Where possible, follow the trodden paths which aid progress through the dense heather and boggy ground. Contour along above the clifftops for the next 2km, crossing several burns cascading down to the cliffs along the way; these are easy enough to cross, but beware of slippery rocks. There is some splendid coastal scenery to admire along this stretch, including impressive cliffs, beautiful bays, waterfalls and rock stacks, with fine views north-east to the Black Cuillin of Skye – conditions permitting.

After 2km Kilmory Lodge – the red deer survey HQ – will come into view. Descend towards a small bay then cut across the open ground in front of **Kilmory Lodge**. Join the Land Rover track that runs to the rear of the lodge. From here you can return to Kinloch via the Land Rover tracks through Kilmory and Kinloch glens or continue along the coast to Samhnan Insir then over Mullach Mòr to join the Kinloch Glen track directly.

Return via Kilmory and Kinloch glens

If you take this option, it is still worth taking some time to explore Kilmory Bay and the coastline as far as Samhnan Insir (see below), before returning to Kilmory. From Kilmory, head south for 4.5km along the Kilmory track before intersecting with the Kinloch–Harris track. Turn left (east) and continue for 3.5km to **Kinloch**.

Return via Mullach Mòr

From Kilmory Lodge follow the track south for 100m before following a vague path east to the **Kilmory River**. If the tide permits cross the river's outflow, otherwise follow it upstream a short way to cross the burn via stepping stones or where safe to do so. Continue beneath the marram grass-covered dunes and onto the beautiful two-tone red-and-white sand expanse of **Kilmory Bay**.

From the eastern end of Kilmory Bay, climb a short way where a sloping outcrop of rock eases up from the beach. Stay just above the shore before descending again to pass a small rocky beach. Continue past a series of remarkable outcrops of weathered Torridonian sandstone, then steer a course around the heads of a couple of narrow gullies. The ground can be quite boggy here, so follow deer

Ruin at Samhnan Insir

tracks across open ground, bearing south-east to reach the western end of the beach at **Samhnan Insir**. Walk along the beautiful sandy beach to the ruined croft house at the south-eastern end of the bay. From here, either retrace your steps to Kilmory Bay, recross the Kilmory River then return to Kinloch via the Landrover tracks through Kilmory and Kinloch glens (see above), or take the following route over Mullach Mòr to join the Kinloch Glen track directly.

Pass the ruined house at the south-eastern end of the bay, cross a gully, climb to the right of several large drystone-walled enclosures and continue directly south up on to the ridge, climbing gently above and east of the Allt Samhnan Insir. The terrain is not rough here and deer paths aid progress through the heather. At around 150m, 1km or so south of Samhnan Insir, contour around a little to the south-west to meet the **Allt Samhnan Insir** and follow the left bank of the burn up through the narrow glen. Where the ground steepens, climb around to the east a little to find the easiest route up through the rocky terrain. Where the ground levels to the east of **Loch Shamhnan Insir**, at around 270m, look out for the 'Vanessa' triangulation pillar atop **Mullach Mòr** (304m) 1km distant to the south-east. Carefully work a route through the terrain of rocky outcrops, small lochans and tussocky grass to the summit, which lies just above and south-east of Boat House Loch.

From the summit, descend initially south-east, then south-west, keeping to the exposed rock of the terraced sandstone ridges tumbling down to **Kinloch Glen** – avoid the terrain between the ridges, which is very hard going through long tussocky grass over uneven ground. Make for the western end of a woodland plantation sitting above the north side of the **Kinloch River**. Follow the deer fence down to a gateway into the plantation and turn left where a boggy footpath contours along through the wooded glen. After about 1km the path intersects a more frequented way, which is part of the north side nature trail. Keep straight ahead, contouring along through the glen for a further 1km before bearing right and descending through a wooden gate. Continue along the edge of a large paddock on a grassy path and then go through another gate. Turn left to reach the **Kinloch** crossroads then right if you're returning to the camping/bunkhouse area or the slipway.

WALK 5 – AROUND THE COAST OF RÙM

The Glen Shellesder burn in spate

WALK 6
Kinloch to Guirdil

Start	Kinloch (NM 402 997)
Finish	Guirdil bothy (NG 319 013)
Time	Kinloch to Guirdil via Bealach a' Bhràigh Bhig 3hr 30min–4hr; Kinloch to Guirdil via Glen Shellesder 2hr 30min–3hr
Distance	Kinloch to Guirdil via Bealach a' Bhràigh Bhig 10.5km (6.5 miles); Kinloch to Guirdil via Glen Shellesder 9.8km (6.1 miles)
Total ascent	via Bealach a' Bhràigh Bhig 415m (1360ft); via Glen Shellesder 295m (970ft)
Difficulty	The tracks and paths are easy to follow for the most part, although the path between Malcolm's Bridge and the Bealach a' Bràigh Bhig can be vague in places. Crossing the Glen Shellesder burn can be dangerous when in spate
Terrain	Metalled track as far as Malcolm's Bridge, rough and often boggy either side of the Bealach a' Bràigh Bhig and through Glen Shellesder
Maps	OS Explorer 397; OS Landranger 39; Harvey Maps, Rùm, Eigg, Canna, Muck Superwalker XT25

This route leads westwards across Rùm to Guirdil, where there is a fine MBA bothy in a remarkable location. This is an excellent base for tackling the hills of western Rùm (Walk 7) or exploring the area's coastline. The alternative, more sheltered route through Glen Shellesder to Guirdil can also be used as a return route for variation. However, in wet weather this route can be very boggy and difficult: there are several fords and attempting to cross the Glen Shellesder burn can be dangerous. The route via the Bealach a' Bhràigh Bhig is the best option both ways in such conditions.

Kinloch to Guirdil via the Bealach a' Bhràigh Bhig
The first section, from Kinloch to the Bealach a' Bhràigh Bhig, takes 2–2hr 30min.

WALK 6 – KINLOCH TO GUIRDIL

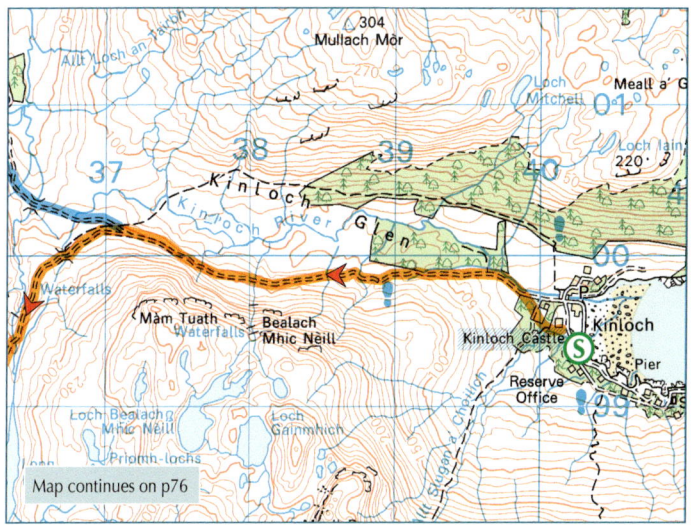

From **Kinloch Castle** (Walk 4), follow the Landrover track north for 200m and turn left to follow the signposted track (8km Kilmory, 13km Harris) west along the south side of the Kinloch River. The **Kinloch Glen** track climbs gradually to 100m then contours along, passing the waterfalls cascading down from Loch Bealach Mhic Nèill after 2.3km. A further kilometre brings you to a fork in the track.

Continue along the left-hand fork. The right-hand track leads to Kilmory Bay and to the alternative route to Guirdil through Glen Shellesder. The track soon passes above the ruins of Salisbury's Dam; the remnants of a failed attempt to improve salmon fishing on the Kinloch River by the second Marquis of Salisbury. The track climbs gradually to 180m and arrives at Malcolm's Bridge 1.75km beyond the Kinloch–Kilmory path junction.

A painted stone on the right-hand side indicates 'Guirdil'. Leave the track here to follow the footpath, originally a pony path, keeping right of the burn and heading initially north along the **Abhainn Monadh Mhiltich**. The path soon trends west, crossing a tributary then later crossing and recrossing the burn – this can be a boggy experience during wet weather, although the path is metalled with stones and old duckboards in some sections. The path begins to climb, gradually at first then more steeply, arriving at the **Bealach a' Braigh Bhig** (370m) after 2.5km. The views are tremendous – the isles of Canna and Sanday lie framed beyond the

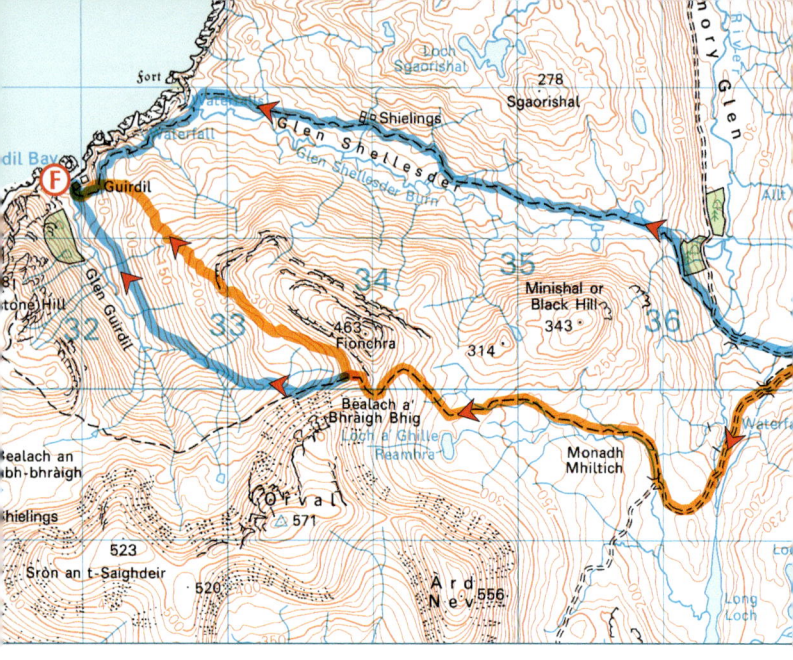

U-shaped mouth of the glen with the distinctive pillow lava-capped summit of Bloodstone Hill rising at its western side.

The easiest route down to Guirdil bothy follows an ATV track that contours along the south-west flank of **Fionchra** before dropping down its north-west ridge to the coast. Follow the old pony path down from the bealach a short way before taking the obvious ATV track off to the right. Lose a little height, ignore tracks off to the left and continue between the gateway formed by a pair of huge, turf-crowned erratic boulders. The track continues contouring along Fionchra's flank for a further 1km before emerging onto the hill's north-west ridge. Continue descending steadily for around 800m before intersecting an old path running along the course of an old drystane dike. Cross over this path and follow the vague trodden paths leading down to where the **Guirdil River** emerges into the bay. Pass through an old iron gateway to reach the **Guirdil bothy** (see Walk 5, Day 2).

Alternative route from the Bealach a' Braigh Bhig to Guirdil via Glen Guirdil
A more scenic route descends through the glen, although this is rougher going. From the bealach, follow the pony path initially north-west (ignore the ATV track that heads off to the right) as it gently descends into, then contours west around the head of **Glen Guirdil**, beneath the towering cliffs of Orval's northern flank.

After around 500m, leave the path and head directly down into the glen. Follow the vague path where possible. After 200m or so, cross a small burn and keep to the right-hand side of a larger burn that feeds into the Guirdil River. After 1km you should pass to the right of a fenced wooded enclosure as the terrain drops more steeply towards the river. When you're level with the bottom corner of the plantation, bear right and contour along on trodden paths. Cross a burn descending a gully at the obvious point and then follow the path running alongside an old, grown-over drystane dike. Continue along the path, which can be boggy in places, for 1km before heading down to **Guirdil Bay** and the bothy. From the bealach to the bothy takes around 1hr–1hr 15min.

To return to Kinloch, retrace your outward route or reverse the outward route via Glen Shellesder – except in very wet weather when this is not a good option.

Alternative route from Kinloch to Guirdil via Glen Shellesder

The walk from Kinloch to the turn-off for this route takes 1hr–1hr 15min (follow the main route description above); the Glen Shellesder path takes 1hr 30min–1hr 45min. At the **Kinloch–Kilmory** Landrover track junction, where the main route to the Bealach a' Bhràigh Bhig forks left, turn right to follow the Kilmory track as it descends a little and soon begins to swing north. After 1km a pair of information posts indicate the 'Kilmory Red Deer Research Area'; join the Glen Shellesder path here – initially a grassy ATV track – which climbs gradually away from the

Heading along the Abhainn Monadh Mhiltich between Malcolm's Bridge and the Bealach a' Bhràigh-bhig

left-hand side (north-east) of the Kilmory track. The path soon passes by a coniferous forestry plantation and after 1km crosses the watershed between Sgaorishal and Minishal at around 135m, before beginning the gradual descent through **Glen Shellesder** The path is quite distinct, but it can be boggy in places and there are several fords, though these are only an issue in wet weather. A ford crosses the river just before it descends to the shore via a waterfall; however, it is often too deep to cross here. Instead, cross 100m upstream – be careful as the rocks are very slippery.

Beneath the cliffs where the Glen Shellesder burn cascades to the shore, there is a remarkable area of coastline full of impressive **geological features** including subterranean tunnels, cavernous caves and a huge rock arch. This area is really worth exploring before you continue on to Guirdil bothy.

The path continues south-west along the coast for 1km and is easy to follow, but it is possible to mislay it before descending to **Guirdil Bay**; however, the **Guirdil bothy** is soon visible below and it is easy to find a route down to it. To return to Kinloch, retrace your outward route or reverse the outward route via the Bealach a' Bhràigh Bhig (see above).

Natural arch north-east of Giurdil Bay

WALK 7
The Guirdil Horseshoe

Start/finish	Guirdil MBA bothy (NG 317 013)
Time	3hr 30min–4hr 30min; including Àrd Nev extension 4hr 30min–5hr 30min
Distance	10.9km (6.8 miles); including Àrd Nev extension 13km (8.1 miles)
Total ascent	888m (2915ft); including Àrd Nev extension 1020m (3350ft)
Difficulty	This is a fairly demanding day's hillwalking on often rough, pathless terrain. Route-finding can be difficult in poor visibility, partly due to lack of paths
Terrain	Except for the walk in, the route is mostly pathless with some rugged and boggy terrain in places. The generally grassy summits of Bloodstone Hill, Orval, Àrd Nev and Fionchra present no difficulties. The descent into Glen Guirdil is boggy and tussocky in places
Maps	OS Explorer 397; OS Landranger 39; Harvey Maps, Rùm, Eigg, Canna, Muck Superwalker XT25

This fine walk takes in some or all of the principal peaks of Rùm's often-overlooked north-west – Bloodstone Hill, Orval, Àrd Nev and Fionchra. Each of these hills has splendid views across Rùm and the neighbouring islands: the views of Canna from Bloodstone Hill and the Rùm Cuillin from Àrd Nev are particularly grand. These whale-backed granite and lava-capped hills are a less demanding proposition than their loftier neighbours dominating the island's southern skyline, although the terrain is rough in places.

The walk into Guirdil bothy from Kinloch via Malcolm's Bridge adds 10.5km each way, or 9.8km each way via Glen Shellesder (Walk 6). Unless you can get a lift or cycle along the Kinloch Glen track to Malcolm's Bridge, walking in and out from Kinloch as well as walking the horseshoe would make for a very long, arduous day. As well as making it more manageable, overnighting at Guirdil bothy – or camping nearby – really adds to the experience of walking this route.

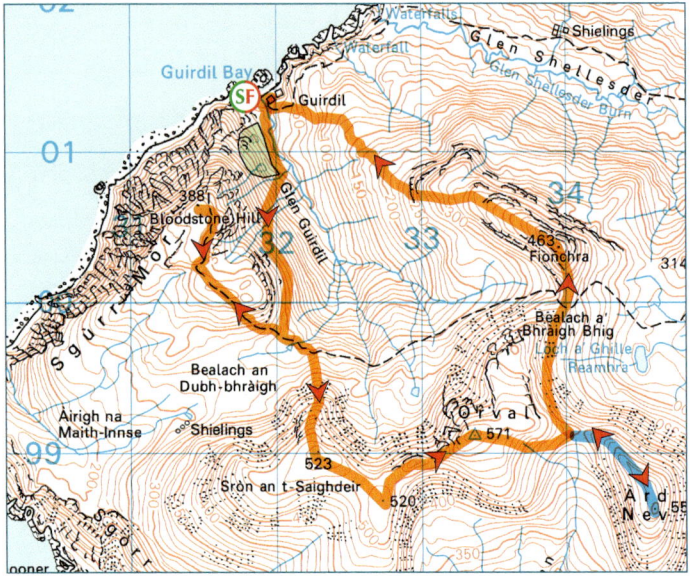

From the bothy, drop down to cross the **Guirdil River** where it is fordable (do not attempt when it is in spate). Head south-east back up the glen next to the river, initially on a track running parallel to a wooded enclosure. At the southeast corner of the enclosure begin climbing steeply up the north-east flank of Bloodstone Hill on a pathless grassy slope. Cross two shallow gullies, continue climbing, then in quick succession cross two burns flowing down gullies at obvious crossing points at around 140m. Continue climbing less steeply to about 220m, then follow traces of an old path, which contours around the hillside, to gain the **Bealach an Dubh-bhràigh** (260m). By a small lochan, join the old pony path that winds around the head of Glen Guirdil between the Bealach a Bhràigh Bhig and **Bloodstone Hill**.

Turn right (north-west) along the pony path and soon begin climbing steadily. The path drops a little to cross an area of boggy ground before climbing again to reach the lava-capped summit. Exercise caution as the summit drops away to sheer cliffs on the hill's north-west flank. The views are spectacular: Canna and Sanday lie supine across the Sound of Canna with Barra and South Uist beyond, while the saw-toothed profile of Skye's Black Cuillin looms to the north-east. Retrace your steps to the bealach.

WALK 7 – THE GUIRDIL HORSESHOE

From the **lochan** on Bealach an Dubh-bhràigh, follow the pony path south-east for around 400m as it skirts around the head of the glen before leaving the track to climb just west of south along the pathless north ridge of Sròn an t-Saighdeir. The 275m climb on an even, steepish gradient on boggy, tussocky, rock-strewn terrain is not the most enjoyable of climbs, but it presents no difficulties. The broad, boulder-strewn plateau of **Sròn an t-Saighdeir** (523m) is marked with a cairn and there are fine views along the ridge to Orval's summit and the Rùm Cuillin to the south. From the cairn, continue south-east then north-east along the grassy ridge, with a little up and down before climbing a short way to the rounded summit of **Orval** (571m), which is marked with a cairn and a trig pillar.

Extension to Àrd Nev
This variant adds 3km to the route and takes around 1hr. Across a bealach to the south-east stands Àrd Nev, a lovely whale-backed hill, which enjoys arguably the best views of the Rùm Cuillin from anywhere on the island. To include Àrd Nev in your itinerary continue east from Orval's summit cairn, soon descending steadily down an even slope with steeply rising ground to your left, arriving on the bealach after 750m. From the bealach, climb directly along the north-west ridge of **Àrd Nev** to arrive at the summit cairn (556m) after a further 750m. Retrace your

Bloodstone Hill rising above Guirdil Bay

steps to the bealach between Àrd Nev and Orval, then contour around the eastern flank of Orval gradually losing height to reach the Bealach a Bhràigh Bhig.

Main route
From Orval's summit, continue north-east then north along the ridge. In clear conditions there are impressive views down Glen Guirdil and along the cliffs of Orval's north-west face. Where the ridge descends to the north it runs into craggy terrain; to avoid this, turn right (east) and descend steeply a short way before bearing north-east to descend to the **Bealach a Bhràigh Bhig** (370m), which is crossed by the pony path between Malcolm's Bridge and Bloodstone Hill. If you're not returning to the bothy you can make an up-and-down ascent of Fionchra, then retrace the outward route from Kinloch (Walk 6).

From the bealach climb steadily north-east for 200m before turning north-west and climbing more steeply to the distinctive cupola-shaped summit of **Fionchra** (463m); the short, straightforward climb takes around 20min. Fionchra provides a good strategic outpost for views across Rùm and beyond, including the towering cliffs forming the north face of Orval.

From the summit, descend north-west directly along the spine of the hill to around 350m. From here, descend more steeply west into Glen Guirdil to avoid the crags above Coire na Loigh. The ground can be hard going until you reach the ATV track contouring along the flank of the hill at around 280m. Follow the track north-westwards along Fionchra's south-western side before emerging onto the hill's north-west ridge. Continue descending steadily for around 800m before intersecting an old path running along the course of an old drystane dike. Cross over this path and follow the vague trodden paths leading down to where the Guirdil River emerges into the bay. Pass through an old iron gateway to reach **Guirdil bothy**.

WALK 8
Orval and Àrd Nev

Start/finish	Kinloch (NM 402 997)
Time	6–6hr 30min
Distance	19.5km (12.1 miles)
Total ascent	850m (2790ft)
Difficulty	The route is straightforward if reasonably demanding in good visibility, although once you're off the Kinloch–Harris track the paths are often vague
Terrain	Good tracks for the walk in and out, generally firm, well-drained hill terrain. Return to Malcolm's Bridge from Bealach a' Bhràigh Bhig can be very boggy at times
Maps	OS Explorer 397; OS Landranger 39; Harvey Maps, Rùm, Eigg, Canna, Muck Superwalker XT25

At 571m, Orval is the principal summit of Rùm's north-west and is well worth a visit for its strategically situated summit ridge, providing magnificent views across the island and beyond. The adjacent summit of Àrd Nev provides easy access to Orval – and Fionchra, which sits just across the Bealach a Bhràigh Bhig, is a quick and easy ascent away.

This route makes for a more manageable tour of Rùm's western hills than Walk 6; enjoying many of the same fine views with fewer kilometres and metres of ascent: a kind of condensed highlights if you will.

The return route along the Kinloch–Harris Landrover track is straightforward to follow and easygoing under foot. The ascent of Àrd Nev and Orval offers no difficulties and the summit of Fionchra can be added to the itinerary with little extra effort. The return along the Abhainn Monadh Mhiltich from the Bealach a Bhràigh Bhig can be very boggy in places at times.

From **Kinloch Castle**, follow the track road north for 200m and turn left to follow the signposted track (8km Kilmory, 13km Harris) west along the south side of the Kinloch River. The **Kinloch Glen** track climbs gradually to 100m then contours along, passing the waterfalls cascading down from **Loch Bealach Mhic Nèill** above the Rocking Stone after 2.3km. A kilometre further brings you to a fork in the track: the right-hand track leads to Kilmory Bay, the left to Harris Bay. Continue

along the left-hand fork. A short way further on the track passes above the ruins of Salisbury's Dam, then continues to climb gradually to arrive at Malcolm's Bridge (180m) 1.75km beyond the Kinloch–Kilmory path junction.

From here the track climbs gradually, reaching its highest point (250m) 1.5km beyond Malcolm's Bridge. Opposite an old quarry, turn right off the track where a gravelled-over culvert heralds the start of an ATV track. Follow this often-boggy track as it climbs westwards up to the bealach between Àrd Nev and Àrd Mheall. Now bear northwards up Àrd Nev's pathless south ridge, which makes for a steeper, but steadier climb than the eastern flank. The summit of **Àrd Nev** (556m) is marked by a small pile-of-stones cairn, which is almost entirely engulfed by vegetation. Àrd Nev enjoys arguably the best panoramic view of the Rùm Cuillin to be had on the island.

WALK 8 – ORVAL AND ÀRD NEV

Descend steadily north-west to the bealach between Àrd Nev and Orval. From here, climb steadily westwards, keeping left of the craggy terrain on Orval's eastern flank. The gradient eases before reaching the rounded summit of **Orval** (571m), which is marked with a cairn and a 'Vanessa' pillar trig point.

From the summit of Orval, continue initially north-west then north along the ridge. In clear conditions there are impressive views down Glen Guirdil and along the cliffs of Orval's west and north-west faces. Where the ridge descends to the north it runs into craggy terrain; to avoid this, turn right (east) and descend steeply a short way before bearing north-east to descend the last 250m to the **Bealach a Bhràigh Bhig** (370m) between Orval and Fionchra. From here you can either return directly to Kinloch or make the short, steep climb of Fionchra.

Àrd Nev seen from Orval

From the bealach climb steadily north then bear north-west to climb more steeply to the distinctive cupola-shaped summit of Fionchra (463m); the short, straightforward climb takes around 15min. Fionchra provides a good strategic outpost for views across Rùm and beyond, including superlative views onto the towering cliffs forming the north-west and west faces of Orval. From the summit of **Fionchra** (463m), descend by the same route to the bealach.

From the bealach descend initially north-east then generally east-south-east along the old pony path, soon crossing the **Abhainn Monadh Mhiltich**, then following its course down towards Malcolm's Bridge. The path, which crosses and recrosses the burn, can be very boggy in places and it is occasionally metalled with stones and old duckboards. On reaching Malcolm's Bridge turn left and follow the track back to **Kinloch** (Walk 4).

WALK 9
Kinloch to Harris Bay

Start/finish	Kinloch (NM 402 997)
Time	5–5hr 30min
Distance	21.5km (13.4 miles)
Total ascent	670m (2200ft)
Difficulty	Straightforward route on clear tracks, although the long return walk on hard ground can be tiring
Terrain	Good, metalled tracks between Kinloch and Harris Bay
Maps	OS Explorer 397; OS Landranger 39; Harvey Maps, Rùm, Eigg, Canna, Muck Superwalker XT25

This is an easy-to-follow route along metalled Landrover tracks for most of its length. While eminently practical, the tracks themselves don't make for inspiring walking though the views of the island's mountainous interior along the way more than make up for this. Harris Bay is a wonderful place to arrive and it's well worth exploring this fine section of Rùm's coastline. The route is also negotiable by mountain bike for much of its length – though the climb out of Harris Bay will involve plenty of pushing. The wildlife-spotting opportunities at Harris Bay are generally very good. There is also a great level, grassy bivouac site down by the shore on the opposite side of the Glen Duian River from the Bullough Mausoleum.

From **Kinloch** follow the track west along the south side of the Kinloch River. The **Kinloch Glen** track climbs gradually to 100m then contours along, passing the waterfalls cascading down from **Loch Bealach Mhic Nèill** after 2.3km. A kilometre further brings you to a fork in the track; the right-hand track leads to Kilmory Bay, the left to Harris Bay.

Continue along the left-hand fork. A short way further on the track passes above the ruins of Salisbury's Dam. The ruins are remnants of a failed attempt to improve salmon fishing on the Kinloch River by the second Marquis of Salisbury. The track climbs gradually to 180m and arrives at Malcolm's Bridge 1.75km beyond the Kinloch–Kilmory path junction. Continuing south-west, the track climbs more steeply to about 250m as it passes beneath the eastern flank and south ridge of Àrd Nev. The track then loses some height before contouring

WALKING RÙM AND THE SMALL ISLES

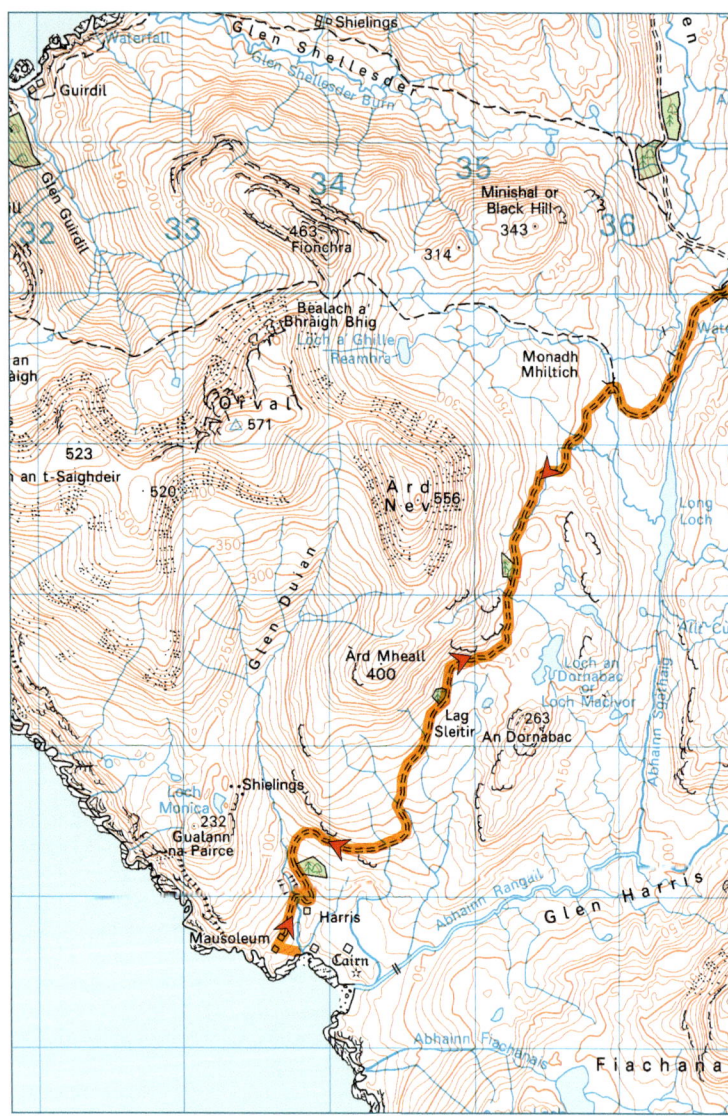

WALK 9 – KINLOCH TO HARRIS BAY

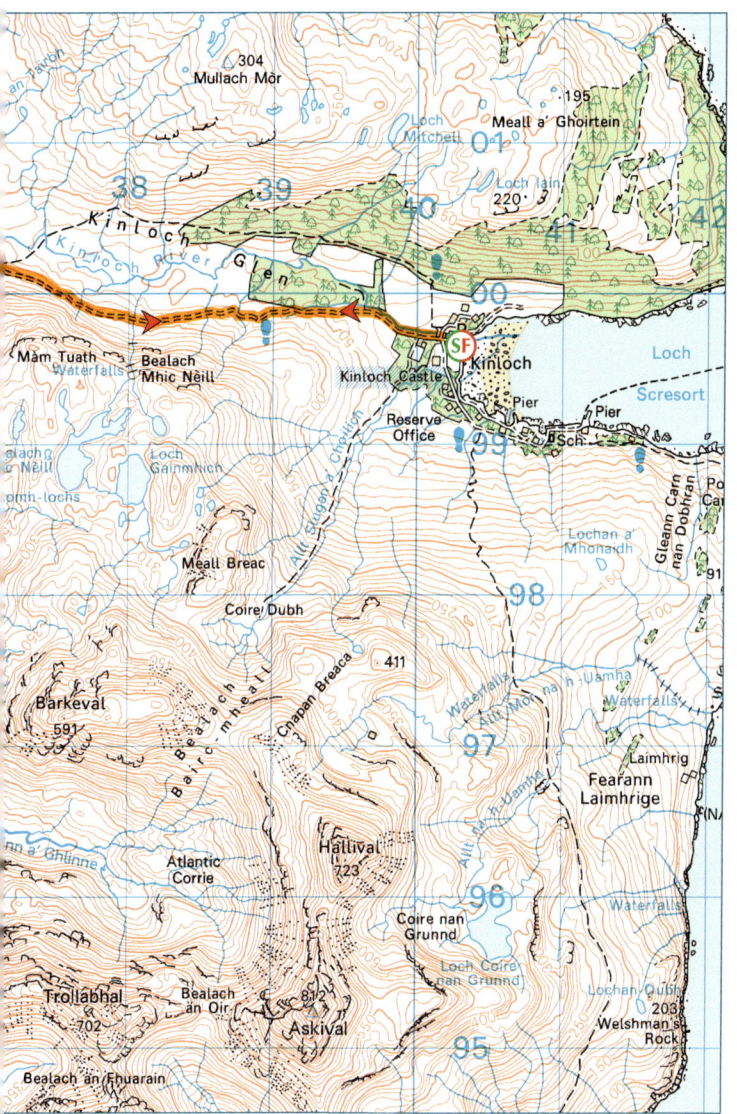

beneath Àrd Mheall then descending more steeply as it winds down to Harris. Cross the bridge over the **Glen Duian River** and continue past the old Harris Lodge to the **Bullough Mausoleum** – a latter-day Greek temple perched above a wild Hebridean shore (see Walk 5, Day 2). Spectacular **Harris Bay**, with its magnificent, raised beach and plentiful wildlife is well worth exploring.

Return to **Kinloch** by your outward route. The 250m climb out of Harris on the way back makes itself felt.

Wild goats at Harris Bay with Ruinsival rising to the south-east

WALK 10
Kinloch to Kilmory Bay

Start/finish	Kinloch (NM 402 997)
Time	5–5hr 30min; including the extension to Samhnan Insir 7–7hr 30min
Distance	16km (9.9 miles); including the extension to Samhnan Insir 20km (12.4 miles)
Total ascent	380m (1245ft); including the extension to Samhnan Insir 470m (1540ft)
Difficulty	A straightforward, relatively undemanding walk, although 16km mostly on firm tracks can be tiring
Terrain	Good, metalled tracks and sandy beach
Maps	OS Explorer 397; OS Landranger 39; Harvey Maps, Rùm, Eigg, Canna, Muck Superwalker XT25

This is a straightforward route following metalled Landrover tracks for most of the way. The tracks themselves would make for dull walking were it not for the fine views of the island's mountainous hinterland along the way. Kilmory Bay, with its two-tone sands, marram grass-thatched dunes and fabulous views, is a wonderful place to spend some time before the return leg of the walk. However, it's well worth exploring further along the coast while you're here. The route is also negotiable by mountain bike or gravel bike as far as Kilmory Lodge.

From **Kinloch**, follow the signposted track (8km Kilmory, 13km Harris) west along the south side of the Kinloch River. The **Kinloch Glen** track climbs gradually to 100m then contours along, passing the waterfalls cascading down from **Loch Bealach Mhic Nèill** after 2.5km. A further 1km brings you to a fork in the track; the right-hand track leads to Kilmory Bay, the left to Harris Bay.

Continue initially west-north-west along the right-hand track, which soon descends a little, crosses the **Kilmory River** on a stone-built bridge, then swings north. After 1km a pair of information posts indicate the 'Kilmory Red Deer Research Area'; the Glen Shellesder path – initially a grassy ATV track – climbs away to the left (north-east) here. Keep straight ahead on the **Kilmory track**, which soon passes coniferous forestry plantations to the left, then right. The track, which is metalled with pebbles for much of its length, is easy to follow as it descends

WALKING RÙM AND THE SMALL ISLES

The remote beach at Samhnan Insir

very gradually over the course of 4.5km to Kilmory Bay. Around 100m before reaching Kilmory Lodge – the base of the joint Edinburgh and Cambridge universities' red deer survey – turn right off the track where a white-painted stone indicates 'Deer Hide' and follow a vague path east to the Kilmory River passing the hide en route. If the tide permits, cross the outflow of the river at the beach, otherwise cross the river a little upstream via stepping stones.

Continue beneath the marram grass-covered dunes and step out along the beautiful two-tone red and white sand expanse of **Kilmory Bay**. On a clear day there are great views north-east to Skye's Black Cuillin. It is worth exploring along the fascinating coastline to the north-east as far as Samhnan Insir, before either returning to **Kinloch** by your outward route, or to make a more challenging circular route by heading over **Mullach Mòr** to Kinloch Glen directly (Walk 5, Day 3).

Extension to Samhnan Insir

The extension to Samhnan Insir is approximately 4km (2.5 miles) return and takes around 2hr. From the eastern end of Kilmory Bay, climb a short way up a smooth outcrop of rock sloping up from the beach. Stay just above the shore before descending again to pass a small rocky beach. Continue past a series of remarkable outcrops of weathered Torridonian sandstone then steer a course around the heads of a couple of narrow gullies. The ground can be quite boggy here, so follow deer tracks across open ground, bearing south-east to eventually reach the western end of the beach at **Samhnan Insir**. Walk along the beautiful sandy beach to the ruined croft house and sheep fanks at the south-eastern end of the bay. From here retrace your steps to Kilmory Bay.

WALK 11
Port na Caranean

Start/finish	Kinloch ferry pier (NM 402 997)
Time	1hr 30min–2hr
Distance	3.3km (2 miles)
Total ascent	100m (330ft)
Difficulty	A shorter, low-level walk, but some rough, boggy ground and slippery rocks require caution
Terrain	Good path through woodland to otter hide, rough and boggy in places thereafter
Maps	OS Explorer 397; OS Landranger 39; Harvey Maps, Rùm, Eigg, Canna, Muck Superwalker XT25

This short walk along the south shore of Loch Scresort to the abandoned settlement of Port na Caranean is full of historical interest and also benefits from outstanding views and great wildlife-spotting opportunities. Despite the maintained gravel path at the start of the walk, don't be lulled into thinking this is an easy stroll suitable for trainers or shoes. Beyond the excellent otter hide the path becomes rough, boggy and overgrown in places – walking boots and gaiters are recommended. It is worth taking binoculars with you to take advantage of the otter hide and also to watch for porpoises, seals and seabirds along the way.

From the **ferry pier** head a short way along the track towards Kinloch then turn left opposite the fish farm shore base onto the path for the otter hide, which is indicated by a marker post with an otter symbol. The gravelled path soon passes a memorial stone to the writer, hillwalker and environmentalist, Irvine Butterfield.

> Irvine Butterfield (1936–2009) was instrumental in the restoration of Dibidil bothy (Walk 5, Day 1) and also wrote a book about it entitled *Dibidil: A Hebridean Adventure*. The back of the memorial stone features a quote from William Blake: 'Great things are done when men and mountains meet; this is not done by jostling in the street'.

WALK 11 – PORT NA CARANEAN

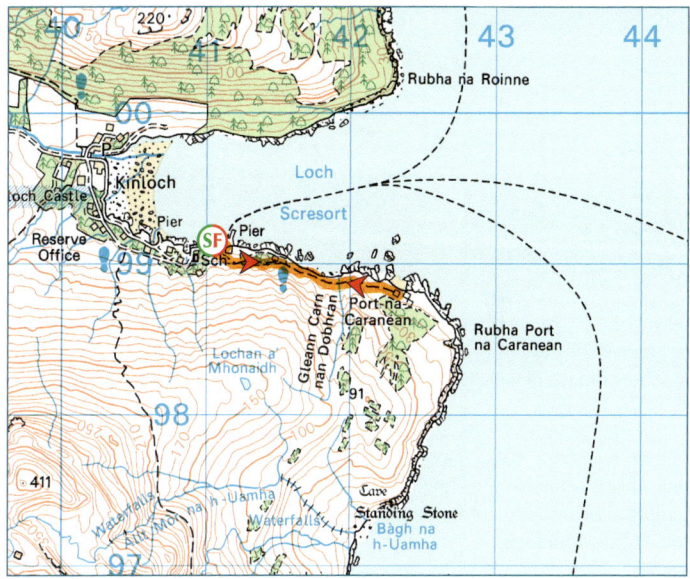

The surfaced path continues into Southside Wood, an enchanting area of native woodland. A short way further on at **Càrn nan dòbhran** (otter stones) the ruins of a couple of houses are encountered among the trees to left and right of the path, their old stones draped in moss. The path soon forks with the onward route to the right and the otter hide to the left at the edge of the woodland overlooking a stony beach. Built in 2008 the hide is a robust timber-framed structure with viewing windows looking out across the shore.

Continuing on from the otter hide, the path initially runs through the bracken skirting the stony shore before leading into the woodland where the way becomes rougher, boggier and less clear in places. The path skirts the pebbly shore at one point before continuing back into the woodland once again and then becomes very unclear as it continues through the trees, climbing and descending a little through the rough, wet, wooded terrain. Just after crossing a small stream, bear right where the more obvious path bears left to continue down through the trees towards the shore again.

The woodland eventually thins out and the path soon crosses open moorland. The going is often boggy underfoot with old duckboards here and there, although some of these have rotted and may be more of a hindrance than a help. Eventually

Walking Rùm and the Small Isles

PORT NA CARANEAN

The township's ruins comprise at least 14 buildings grouped into several farmsteads, including six houses, several byres and small enclosures as well as a drystane head-dike, which can be traced for at least 300m as it runs to the rear of the farmsteads. Port na Caranean was settled by several families of crofters cleared from Bracadale on Skye in the 1820s. The land was less than ideal for cultivation and crofting here proved difficult; by the 1850s most of these families had emigrated to Canada and by 1860 the last inhabitants had abandoned the settlement and moved to Kinloch.

the path briefly passes through another wooded area with rowan, alder and sessile oak to reach the extensive ruins of **Port na Caranean** a short way above the shore. In summer much of the abandoned settlement is engulfed by high bracken.

In clear conditions there are tremendous views north-eastwards to Skye's Cuillin mountains, rising beyond the isle of Soay. Weather and midges permitting, this is a fine spot to linger, absorbing the views, observing the island's birdlife and watching out for otters, seals and porpoises. Retrace your outward route back to **Kinloch**.

Ruins at Port na Caranean, looking out across the sound to the Cuillin Hills of Skye

EIGG

Walkers atop the summit of An Sgùrr (Walk 14)

An Sgùrr looms beyond Galmisdale Bay (Walk 12)

EIGG

Eigg, second largest of the Small Isles, lies a little less than 7km south-east of Rùm, 11km to the south of Skye, and 7.5km north of the Ardnamurchan peninsula. The island is 9km from north to south, 5km east to west and has an area of 31km². Eigg boasts the most varied scenery of the Small Isles and also has a diverse range of wildlife habitats. Community-owned, the island is managed in partnership with the Scottish Wildlife Trust (SWT), with the remit of nurturing the indigenous flora and fauna and increasing the island's biodiversity in the long term.

Eigg's obvious draw for walkers is An Sgùrr, the island's distinctive pitchstone summit, which is sheer on three sides and rises to 393m. In clear conditions the summit of An Sgùrr provides fine 360-degree views, taking in the surrounding islands and the mountains of the mainland. However, there is more to walking on Eigg than An Sgùrr alone. The routes in this guide traverse a range of landscapes including a moorland plateau, white-sand bays, basalt cliffs, rocky coastline and abandoned settlements.

Eigg is the historic capital of the Small Isles Parish and has the largest population of the island group, with 138 permanent residents in 2022 – consequently, it has more accommodation and amenities than the other three Small Isles. The fertile pastures, sheltered bays and mild climate have long marked Eigg as an attractive site for settlement, with human occupation of the island dating back 8000 years. However, Eigg's history has often been bloody and turbulent with massacres, forced migration and feckless owners visited on the islanders over the centuries.

The community's fortunes have improved since the island was bought by the Isle of Eigg Heritage Trust (IEHT), a partnership of islanders, the Highland Council and the SWT. With the buy-out in 1997, the islanders took control of their future, bringing to a close decades of mismanagement by absentee landlords. Notably, the Eigg community has become a hotbed of environmental endeavour, implementing successful sustainable energy production and biodiversity development. The harbour, pier, ferry terminal and main anchorage are situated at Galmisdale, in the island's south-east corner. The grocery shop, post office, craft shop and café/restaurant are all located near the pier and several scatterings of houses are found in the vicinity at Galmisdale, Sandamhor and Kildonan. The main settlement is Cleadale, a fertile coastal plain on the island's northwest coast.

The centre of Eigg is a moorland plateau, rising to 393m (1289ft) at An Sgùrr, the island's distinctive, prow-like pitchstone summit. In fine weather, the summit of An Sgùrr offers spectacular 360-degree views of Rùm, Coll, Muck, the Outer Hebrides, Skye, Ardnamurchan and the mountains of mainland Lochaber.

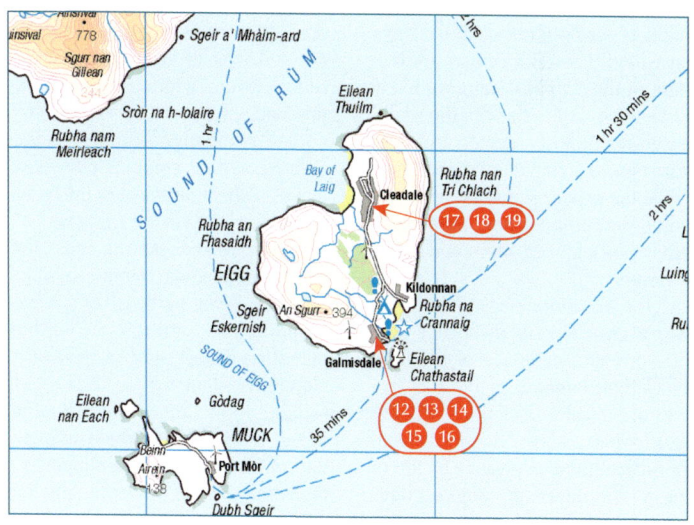

Galmisdale Bay (Walk 12)

GEOLOGY

Eigg and its neighbour, Muck, are both largely formed of lava flows of the Tertiary Period, which are the remnants of what was once a much larger lava field. These lava flows are evident in the step-like features clearly visible on both islands; the small escarpments were formed from the hard, slow-cooling core of each flow, while the gentler slopes between are composed of the softer, more easily eroded rock formed above and below the core.

The pitchstone ridge of An Sgùrr, which gives Eigg its distinctive profile, provides evidence of the final phases of volcanic activity in this area of Scotland. Thick flows of basalt lava formed a harsh and inhospitable landscape. Lying in a valley on top of these lavas, layers of conglomerates containing water-rounded pebbles reveal the course of an ancient riverbed.

As volcanic activity in the area drew to a close, a nearby volcano erupted lava of an unusual, sticky composition, which flowed along this ancient water course. The lava cooled gradually, forming remarkable hexagonal columns dozens of metres high, reminiscent of the basalt columns of the Giant's Causeway on Northern Ireland's Antrim coast and Fingal's Cave on the Hebridean island of Staffa. Being harder than the surrounding rock, erosion has left the pitchstone eminence of An Sgùrr in its elevated position.

The formation of the extensive inland cliff round the whole northern part of Eigg is due to the slipping of the basalt mass of Beinn Bhuidhe on the underlying sediments. Beneath the basalts are a series of sandstones, limestones and shales formed during the Jurassic period. These form the low ground running round the coast from Kildonan in the south-east to Laig in the north-west.

Glaciation removed much of the pre-glacial soil from the island, except for small quantities of boulder clay. However, rapid weathering of the basalt rock combined with wind-blown sand has produced excellent loam soils, albeit deficient in phosphate. The phenomenon of the 'singing sands' of Tràigh a' Bhìgeil at Cleadale is attributable to the uniform size of the quartz grains which form them: the sands only 'sing' when dry.

HISTORY

Neolithic axe heads have been recovered on Eigg and burial cairns span the long period between the Neolithic and Bronze Ages. Several Bronze Age farms provide evidence of continuing settlement, and there are a number of Iron Age duns (forts) on the island, including one impressively located on An Sgùrr and another at Rubha na Crannaig.

Towards the end of the sixth century a monastery was founded at Kildonan by St Donnan, a Celtic Christian missionary from Ireland. However, Donnan's presence eventually provoked the wrath of the local Pictish queen, who massacred the entire monastic community in 617.

St Donnan is believed to have been buried on the island. After his death, the monastery came under Iona's rule and subsequently flourished. Several Early Christian crosses recovered at Kildonan attest to the monastery's importance at the time..

Eigg was subjected to Viking raids from early in the eighth century, but the Norsemen eventually settled here and used the island as a base for trading with Ireland and beyond. As well as physical traces – including the remains of a boat that was uncovered as the sand washed away at Laig Bay and a sword found at Kildonnan – evidence of the Norse settlement is apparent in island place names, such as Galmisdale, Cleadale and

The impressive entrance to Uamh Chràbhaichd (Walk 12)

'Eigg' itself, which derives from an Old Norse word meaning 'hollow' or 'notch', referring to the island's low-lying middle.

By the Middle Ages, the island was in the hands of the MacDonalds of Clanranald, the Lords of the Isles. Eigg lay at the heart of the Clanranald territory and the island's population found itself embroiled in each of the MacDonald rebellions against the Crown, as well as various clan feuds. In 1577 the MacLeods of Dunvegan massacred Eigg's community in the cave of Uamh Fhraing (see Walk 12 for this grisly tale and how to find the cave).

Just over a decade later, in 1588, Eigg – along with the other Small Isles – was sacked by Lachlan Maclean of Duart, who led a raiding party, including 100 Spanish marines from a galleon of the defeated Armada lying at Tobermory. The raiders burnt the islands' settlements and murdered many of the islanders, sparing neither women nor children.

The islanders paid a high price for following their clan chiefs during the Jacobite Rebellions of 1715 and 1745. After the failure of the 1745 rebellion, the chief of Clanranald escaped to France, having first taken refuge in a cave at the north end of Eigg. The islanders who had followed him were captured by the Royal Navy, taken to London and tried. Nineteen of their number died in prison, 18 were transported to Jamaica and only two returned.

Towards the end of the 18th century, the island sustained a population of some 500 people, producing potatoes, oats, black cattle and kelp. The harvesting of kelp, which was used in the production of glass, financed construction of the island's main farmhouses, which were tenanted by old Clanranald families, until the clan chiefs raised rents exponentially, causing many islanders to emigrate to Canada.

In the mid-19th century, the Clearances were imposed upon many parts of the Highlands and Islands when sheep farming became more profitable. Higher prices were offered for land empty of people, where sheep could be pastured. On Eigg, the townships of Grulin under the Sgùrr were evicted in 1853; of the 14 families who lived there, only two found homes elsewhere on the island, while 12 were sent to Canada. The stone ruins of their houses (Walks 13 and 14) are testament to that bleak period of Highland history.

In 1896 Eigg was bought by Lawrence Thomson, who had made his fortune selling warships to Japan. His wealth helped to maintain the estate at a high level and the islanders' lot was generally improved under his stewardship. Thomson died in 1913 and the island passed to his brother before changing hands several times over a short period.

In 1925, the island was purchased by Sir Walter Runciman, a wealthy shipowner and President of

Rùm beyond Cleadale from Sgorr an Fharaidh (Walk 17)

the Board of Trade. Lord Runciman built The Lodge and its exotic gardens and used the island as a recreational and sporting estate. Despite not being resident, he initiated an extensive programme of improvements to the island's infrastructure.

During the Second World War, Laig Bay by Cleadale was used by commandos training for the Normandy landings, while many islanders served in the Royal Navy with several seeing action in the Atlantic Convoys. In the post-war world of austerity, economic conditions changed and – even though the island was efficiently run as one hill farm – it was no longer profitable. The subsequent sale of Eigg in 1966 was prelude to a long period of instability, with successive owners who did little to maintain the island community.

After decades of problems with absentee landlords, the island was bought in 1997 by the Isle of Eigg Heritage Trust, a partnership between the islanders, the Highland Council and the Scottish Wildlife Trust. A ceremony to mark the handover to community ownership took place on 12 June 1997, with a 60-million-year-old lava pillar erected at the pier to commemorate the auspicious day.

WILDLIFE

The largest wild land mammal on Eigg is the otter, which can be found all around the coastline. Rabbits are abundant. The island wood mouse is said to originate from the Norse settlement, reputedly arriving in Viking longships. Short-tailed voles are very common, long-tailed field mice and pygmy shrews less so. Bats also occur on the island, including a sizeable pipistrelle colony and a few long-eared bats.

Insect life is plentiful and varied; butterflies occur in abundance during the summer months and the island's 18 species include speckled woods, dark green and small pearl-bordered fritillaries, and the green hairstreak. In recent years, migrant species have included orange tips, peacock, painted lady and occasional clouded yellows. Nine species of damselfly and dragonfly have been recorded on the island. The friendless midge and the cleg – an aggressive horse fly – do occur on Eigg, but in nothing like the numbers suffered on Rùm. Toads are present, as are common lizards and palmate newts. Adders do not occur.

Both common and grey seals are numerous around the island, particularly on skerries near the harbour at Galmisdale and Eilean Thuilm at the north end. Minke whales are regularly seen in the waters around the island between July and September. Dolphins of several species and porpoises are common, and killer whales (orca) are occasionally spotted. The basking shark is a seasonal visitor, feeding in Eigg's rich coastal waters.

An average of 130 species of bird are recorded annually on Eigg. The island has breeding populations of various raptors: golden eagle, white-tailed eagle, buzzard, peregrine falcon, sparrowhawk, kestrel, hen harrier, barn owl and short- and long-eared owls. Eigg has areas of mature woodland and high heather moorland providing habitat for tits, goldcrests, willow-warblers, siskins, flycatchers and bullfinches, among other species. Hooded crows are present in numbers and several pairs of ravens nest on the island. The elusive corncrake has also been recorded in recent years.

Seabirds are less common than on neighbouring islands and are found mostly at the north end of Eigg. Puffins, guillemots, razorbills and kittiwakes are seen offshore, while fulmars nest on the south cliffs and Manx shearwaters on the inland cliffs by Cleadale. Cormorants, shags, herring and common gulls, great and lesser black-backed gulls are also present.

Both golden and white-tailed eagles can be seen around the island's cliffs

Just north of the school, this is thought to be a 19th-century commemorative stone standing in the place of an ancient cross (Walks 15 and 16)

Red-throated and great northern divers, red-breasted merganser, eider, shelduck, teal, widgeon, golden eye, oystercatcher, golden and ringed plovers, sanderling, curlew, snipe and sandpiper are among the divers, ducks and waders to be found on Eigg. Passage migrants are numerous and some may overwinter, including waxwings, turnstones and bar-tailed godwits, greylag, white-fronted, pink-footed, barnacle and brent geese.

WOODLAND, PLANTS AND FLOWERS

Most of Eigg's central plateau is heather-covered. Grassland on the lower-lying ground is overrun by bracken in some areas. Natural woodland is fairly extensive around Galmisdale, and there are sizeable areas of forestry plantation to the west of the road between Galmisdale and Cleadale. Several exotic species, including eucalyptus, are found in the grounds of The Lodge in the north-west of Galmisdale.

Eigg has been called the 'isle of flowers' by naturalists; its rich and varied plant life includes 500 higher plant species and a bryophyte list numbering well over 300 species, of which over 20 are national rarities. A good deal of the island is covered in hazel scrub woodland, so blue-bells, wild garlic, wood anemone, wood sorrel and primroses abound in spring. Later, in the summer, they are replaced by honeysuckle, enchanter's nightshade and many other species. Twelve species of orchid grow on the island, including the often-abundant heath spotted, fragrant and northern marsh orchids. Scarcer species are great butterfly, small white and frog orchids.

The island's cliffs are home to a good cross section of Alpine and Arctic species, particularly on the edges and ledges of the cliffs to the west of Beinn Bhuidhe: cushion pink, globe flowers, mountain avens, both purple and yellow saxifrage, moss campion and the rare Arctic sandwort. Ferns are abundant too, and include species such as rusty bark, adder's-tongue and the odd-looking moonwort.

GETTING AROUND

With the exception of Blue Badge holders, visitors are not allowed to bring vehicles to Eigg, and there is no public transport on the island. Getting around on foot is the norm for most visitors, but bicycles are useful along the island's few kilometres of road. As well as kayak hire, Eigg Adventures (tel 01687 347007 www.eiggadventures.co.uk), located at the pierside An Laimhrig complex, provide mountain bike and e-bike rental; if you have trouble with your own bike, Owain (who runs the operation) also offers an emergency repair service and a selection of spare parts.

The Eigg Taxi is operated by Charlie (tel 01687 482404).

AMENITIES

The Isle of Eigg's website (http://isleofeigg.org) provides regularly updated information regarding amenities, accommodation and transport. Be sure to check current opening times online before relying on a service.

The exceptionally well-stocked Isle of Eigg shop (tel 01687 482432) is part of the small An Laimhrig pierside complex; pre-ordering and a delivery service can be arranged. The post office is in the shop and has a cash-withdrawal facility.

Galmisdale Bay (tel 01687 482487 https://galmisdale-bay.com) café, bar and restaurant is situated next to the shop and provides meals and snacks using locally sourced and produced food.

Also part of the pierside complex, Taigh Nighe (the Wash House; open 24/7) has toilets, paid showers, a laundry and a drying room, while the Isle of Eigg craft shop sells local arts and crafts, as well as pamphlets on Eigg's geology, history and wildlife.

In the middle of the island, just north of the school, the tiny Isle of Eigg Brewery (www.eiggbrewery.com) is Scotland's first cooperative brewery and is open for tastings and tours some afternoons in summer.

Fine dining is available at the Lageorna Restaurant (tel 01687 460081 www.lageorna.com) in Cleadale – advance booking only.

At Rest and Be Thankful – in Cleadale – tea, coffee and homemade cake are served in a gazebo in the garden. The tiny operation's summer-only opening hours are variable.

PLACES TO STAY

Glebe Barn (tel 01687 315099 www.glebebarn.co.uk) provides 22 beds in a spacious bunkhouse 1.5km from the pier. The accommodation is comfortable and well-equipped with a large communal area for sitting and dining, a bright conservatory with tremendous views to the mainland and a pretty garden. The attached Glebe Apartment (sleeps two) has a sleeping mezzanine and private entrance.

At Galmisdale Bay, the community-owned Eigg Camping Pods (www.eiggcampingpods.com; open March–December) has three pods, each sleeping four and each with a small heater, fridge, kettle and lighting. You must bring your own bedding and cooking equipment. Galmisdale Bay café, bar and restaurant is a short walk away, as is the shop.

In Cleadale, Eigg Organics (tel 07482 622122 www.eiggorganics.co.uk) has camping with basic facilities and outstanding views, as well as basic self-catering accommodation at Cleadale Bothy (sleeps 4), which includes a cooker, wood-burning stove and bedding, with outdoor composting toilets.

The most upmarket option is Lageorna (tel 01687 460081 www.lageorna.com; two rooms) in Cleadale, providing B&B accommodation attached to its small, highly regarded restaurant (see above), which is also open to non-residents with advance booking. Packed lunches are also available.

The island additionally has extensive self-catering options; listings can be found at www.isleofeigg.org/accommodation.

An Sgùrr's southern face shows off the remarkable pitchstone ridge to dramatic effect (Walks 13 and 14)

WALK 12
Uamh Fhraing and Uamh Chràbhaichd

Start/finish	Galmisdale pier (NM 484 838)
Time	1hr 15min
Distance	3.5km (2.2 miles)
Total ascent	150m (490ft)
Difficulty	An easy walk with some care needed on coastal rocks
Terrain	Tracks, grassy fields and rocky shoreline
Maps	OS Explorer 397; OS Landranger 39; Harvey Maps, Rùm, Eigg, Canna, Muck Superwalker XT25

This short, undemanding coastal walk visits two caves: firstly, Uamh Fhraing, a haunting site where nearly 400 people were massacred in the 16th century; then, an optional, tide-dependent extension to the cavernous Uamh Chràbhaichd. Along the way, lapwings swoop over fertile fields in season with views across the water to Eilean Chathastail, while the final section follows a rocky shoreline below cliffs with Muck lying supine across the horizon.

From **Galmisdale Bay**, follow the left-hand road fork heading north-west uphill, passing some camping pods on your right. Continue for around 600m through mature sycamore trees. Ignore the turning on the right towards the Community Hall, then, shortly afterwards, look for a gatepost (NM 479 840) on your left marked with a small yellow arrow and a pink circle. Go through this gateway onto a substantial track and continue to a second gate. Pass through this then, just before you reach a house, leave the main track and continue along a grassy track on the left that heads south with the house initially on your right-hand side.

Follow this track through fields of grass and wild flowers for 500m as it trends from south to south-west and then west below some rocky crags, until eventually it splits and becomes less distinct as it approaches a small metal gate. Go through this gate and follow a narrower path leading straight ahead with cliffs and the sea beyond a fence on your left-hand side. Soon, the path reaches two wooden gateposts at the start of a series of steps that descend towards the shore. Walk down the steps then, where the path forks, bear left to reach the narrow entrance to **Uamh Fhraing** in the cliffs here (NM 475 835). A sign now advises against exploring its dark, dank recesses due to the risk of falling rocks.

The low cliffs of the south coast where both caves are hidden

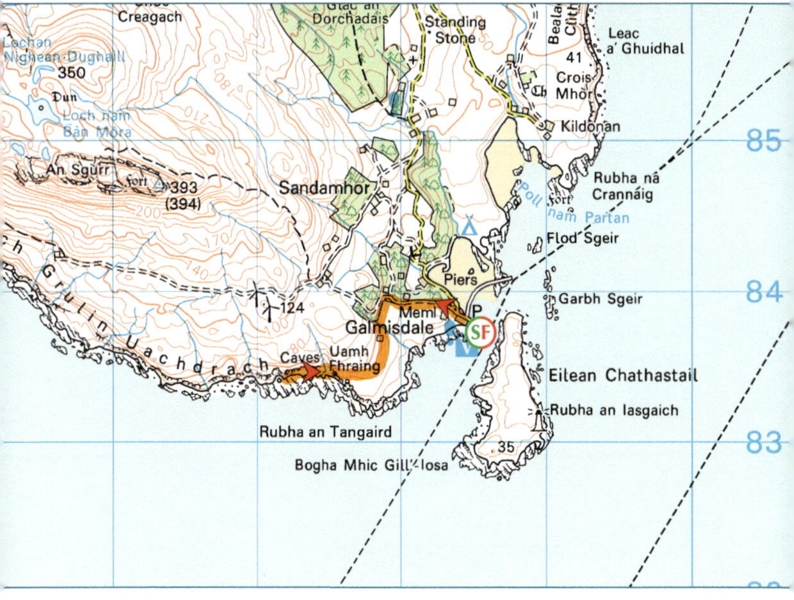

From here, if the tide is low and you want to continue to **Uamh Chràbhaichd** (Cathedral Cave), clamber over the shoreline rocks or follow a small path beneath the cliffs 300m west – the gaping cavern mouth is impossible to miss.

It's said that in 1843, when hundreds of ministers left the Church of Scotland to form the Free Church, the high-roofed **Uamh Chràbhaichd** was used to host services because the new ministers and congregations were not allowed to use Church of Scotland property.

To return to **Galmisdale Bay** head back to the steps beside Uamh Fhraing and retrace your outward route.

UAMH FHRAING

Commonly referred to as the Massacre Cave, Uamh Fhraing has been a rather morbid tourist attraction since the 19th century when its murky interior still held decomposed bodies. Eventually, this led the people of Eigg to remove the corpses for proper Christian burials.

The cave's tale is one set in a wider context of clan warfare: a story of revenge, where ordinary people were collateral damage in a feud between the MacDonalds of Clanranald and MacLeods of Dunvegan. Its hazy narrative begins on Eilean Chathastail, the small island opposite Galmisdale Bay, where in 1577 a group of women who were tending to cattle there were 'abused' by a group of MacLeod men on their way back to Skye from Glasgow. In retaliation, the offenders were killed by the women's Eigg kinsmen, an extension of the MacDonald clan.

The feud continued as a larger party of MacLeods returned to Eigg to avenge these deaths. However, the raiders' ship was spotted and the island's inhabitants – a reported 395 people – crushed into Uamh Fhraing to hide. Legend tells that after a while a scout was sent out; this unfortunate man was captured just as the invaders were setting sail to leave and, with fresh snow on the ground, his footprints betrayed the way back to the cave. With only one exit route, the Eigg families were trapped as the MacLeods built a huge fire, blocking the small entrance to the cave, which filled with smoke and suffocated those inside. The island's population was all but eradicated.

This string of atrocities continued in a bloody and protracted feud. Life could be perilous for ordinary folk in the times of clan warfare when the communities of small islands and isolated peninsulas were very much at the mercy of the all-powerful clan chiefs' whims.

Inside Uamh Fhraing (photographed in 2019)

WALK 13
Grulin from Galmisdale

Start/finish	Galmisdale pier (NM 484 838)
Time	2–3hr
Distance	9km (5.6 miles)
Total ascent	200m (655ft)
Difficulty	With good tracks or trodden paths the whole way, this route presents no difficulties
Terrain	Tracks and grassy paths
Maps	OS Explorer 397; OS Landranger 39; Harvey Maps, Rùm, Eigg, Canna, Muck Superwalker XT25

Following a once-cultivated plateau between the imposing southern face of An Sgùrr and the low cliffs of Eigg's south-west coast, this undemanding walk visits the ruins of pre-Clearance settlements at Grulin Uachdrach and Grulin Iochdrach (Upper and Lower Grulin), the most extensive of their kind in the Small Isles. With simple navigation and a good track most of the way, this out-and-back route makes for a rewarding excursion the morning before an afternoon ferry or on a day with less than perfect weather.

From **Galmisdale pier**, follow the left-hand road fork, which climbs gently north-west and soon enters woodland. Keep straight on, bearing left after 500m (the right fork leads to the village hall). A little further on, a left-hand turn leads ultimately to Uamh Fhraing (a worthwhile detour on the return, see Walk 12); keep straight on, following a track that climbs steadily before emerging from the woods through a gate into a grassy field with An Sgùrr now dominating the horizon. Follow the track, which leads up across the field towards **Galmisdale House** and pass through a gate on its right-hand side. Turn left onto another track.

> Dramatically positioned beneath An Sgùrr, **Galmisdale House** has served as a post office, inn, factor's house, shooting lodge, the proprietor's residence and – in the early 1800s – a tacksman's house, improved by profits from the kelp industry.

WALK 13 – GRULIN FROM GALMISDALE

One building at Grulin Uachdrach has been restored

GRULIN UACHDRACH

There are traces of at least 42 ruined buildings in Grulin Uachdrach alone with a further 17 in Grulin Iochdrach. With some above and some below the track, in various stages of dilapidation, they span several generations of families through the 18th and mid-19th centuries. The 1841 census shows all of Upper Grulin's inhabitants to have been crofters or herdsmen, suggesting an entirely agriculture-based economy. In 1853, in scenes repeated throughout the Highlands and Islands, the communities were evicted in favour of more profitable sheep farming. Of the 14 families who lived between Grulin Uachdrach and Grulin Iochdrach, 12 were sent to Nova Scotia, while the remaining two made lives in other parts of Eigg.

Follow this track west for 2km, walking below the sheer cliffs which form the imposing southern face of An Sgùrr, until you reach the ruined settlement of **Grulin Uachdrach** (Upper Grulin).

From here, follow a grassy path leading roughly west-north-west then north-west for a further 1.5km to reach the neighbouring township of **Grulin Iochdrach**.

Meaning 'stony place', **Grulin** is associated with a mythical battle between two giants – Husdal and Nuallan – with the peculiar boulders scattered around the area said to be remnants of their struggle.

To return to **Galmisdale pier** retrace your outward steps.

WALK 14
An Sgùrr and Grulin

Start/finish	Galmisdale pier (NM 484 838)
Time	An Sgùrr and Grulin 4–5hr; An Sgùrr return 3–3hr 30min
Distance	An Sgùrr and Grulin 11.5km (7.1 miles); An Sgùrr return 8.3km (5.2 miles)
Total ascent	An Sgùrr and Grulin 415m (1360ft); An Sgùrr return 370m (1215ft)
Difficulty	Although it involves some ascent, climbing An Sgùrr is fairly straightforward; the section between An Sgùrr and Grulin requires careful navigation and can be arduous over rough ground – an easy return along tracks
Terrain	Boggy in places on the approach to An Sgùrr; pitchstone provides good grip underfoot on the summit ridge; rough, heathery ground between An Sgùrr and Grulin
Maps	OS Explorer 397; OS Landranger 39; Harvey Maps, Rùm, Eigg, Canna, Muck Superwalker XT25

An unsurpassed vantage point for magnificent views of Rùm, Coll, Muck, the Outer Hebrides, Skye, Ardnamurchan and the mountains of Lochaber, the towering pitchstone monolith of An Sgùrr is visible from far and wide. Climbing An Sgùrr from Galmisdale makes for a fine half-day walk – a good leg-stretcher, though not especially challenging. However, walking along the summit ridge makes for a stimulatingly exposed sensation, and the world drops away on three sheer cliff-faced sides at the actual summit. Continuing on to the ruins of the Grulin cleared villages from An Sgùrr makes for a very worthwhile extension to this route, though route-finding can be tricky as the vague paths are hard to follow in places and some awkward terrain is traversed.

From **Galmisdale pier**, take the road heading north-west (left), passing some camping pods on your right. Follow the road for 500m, climbing through woodland, ignore the right turn to the community hall and continue straight on (bearing left). After 30m, a left-hand turn leads to Uamh Fhraing (Walk 12), but keep straight on, following the track uphill, before emerging from the woods through a gate into a grassy field with the imposing sight of The Nose, An Sgùrr's eastern

WALKING RÙM AND THE SMALL ISLES

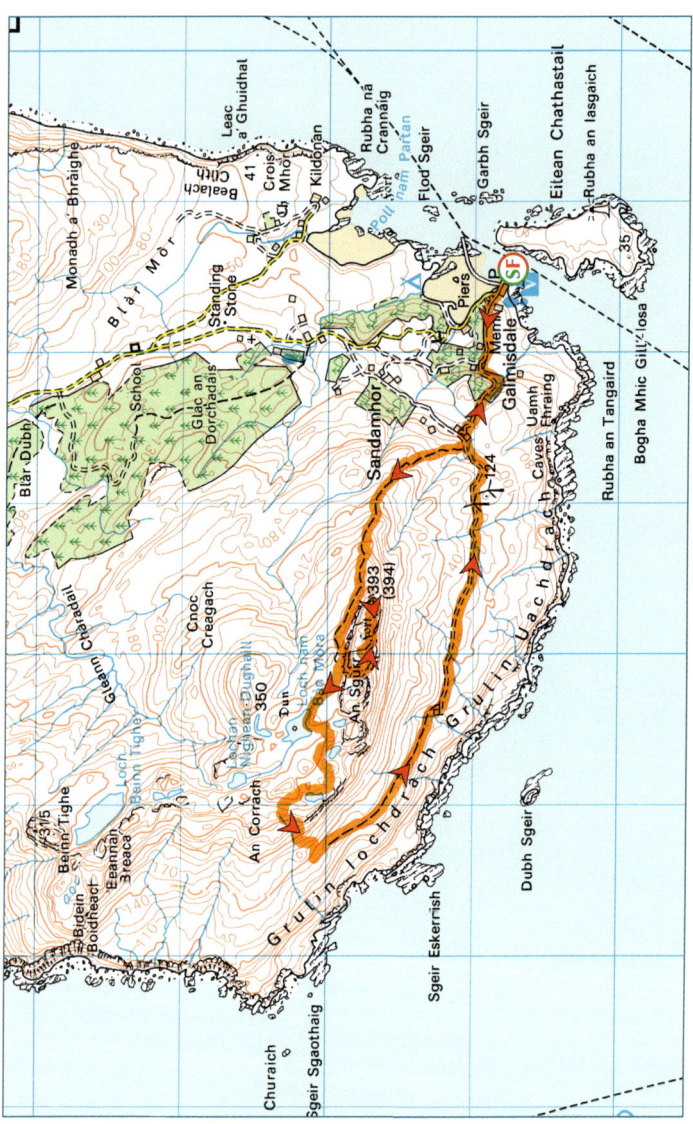

WALK 14 – AN SGÙRR AND GRULIN

face now ahead. Follow the track up across the field towards a house and pass through a gate on its right-hand side. Turn left onto a track and, after 80m, a cairn marks the turning to a well-trodden path to An Sgùrr on the right (NM 474 841).

Looking up at An Sgùrr's intimidating, columnar cliffs from the south-eastern approach, the 393m hill looks to be the preserve of rock climbers, but the route up from the north is untechnical and surprisingly straightforward.

Take this path, which climbs past **An Sgùrr**'s eastern face, before traversing beneath the northern flank of the summit ridge as the gradient slackens underfoot. The path soon turns south, climbing steeply up through an obvious gully to a narrow grassy saddle across the spine of the ridge. From here there are great views north-west over Loch nam Ban Mòra to the Rùm Cuillin, and south across to Muck and down onto the ruins of Grulin. The remains of a few red-paint waymarkers lead you east (left) up onto the exposed rock of the summit ridge, then continue for 500m to reach the summit, which is marked by a cylindrical 'Vanessa' triangulation pillar. On a clear day the views are stunning and the sheer drop on three sides makes for an airy sensation. Descend by the same route. To return to Galmisdale, simply retrace your outward steps.

To continue on to Grulin, descend as far as the foot of the northern flank of the summit ridge beneath the gully. From here, look for a faint trodden path heading west-north-west. Follow this to the south-eastern end of **Loch nam Ban Mòra** across heathery, boggy ground. Skirt the south-east shore of the loch on a vague

Approaching An Sgùrr beneath The Nose

LOCH NAM BAN MÒRA

Saint Donnán, a contemporary of Columba, is said to have been martyred on Eigg in the year 617. Several contradictory legends describe the series of events, but the most imaginative explains how the Pictish queen sent her warrior women to kill Donnán and his monks. After beheading them, the women saw lights shining above the dead and heard enchanting voices. Entranced, they were led by the lights up towards An Sgùrr and into Loch nam Ban Mòra (Loch of the Great Women) where they drowned.

path for 170m until you begin to approach its most southerly point. The circular islet by Loch nam Ban Mòra's northern shore was used as the foundation for a prehistoric *dùn*.

From here head directly south (you might be able to follow a vague path) over an area of lower ground until you're standing above a beautiful **lochan** tucked beneath the Sgùrr. Bear right (west) and follow lengths of path where available, passing north of a **second lochan** and continuing until you reach the eastern shore of a **third lochan**. Walk north just above the eastern shoreline of the third lochan and then head north-west some 220m until you're clear of An Sgùrr's crags before beginning to descend south-west to Grulin Iochdrach.

The way down can be awkward as there is dense heather cover to negotiate, but it involves no real hazard. Pick a good line of descent from above and make a gradual traverse rather than dropping directly – the stone ruins should soon be visible below.

At the foot of the slope, after taking a look around **Grulin Iochdrach** (see Walk 13 for more information), follow a distinct path leading south-east to **Grulin Uachdrach** where you will find a track. Continue in an easterly direction, following the track, which contours along beneath the Sgùrr with fine views of its impressive south face, until, after 1.8km, you reach the cairn-marked turn-off to An Sgùrr. Continue on the track for a further 80m, then turn right through a gate and retrace your outward route back to **Galmisdale**.

WALK 15
Beannan Breaca and the south-west

Start/finish	Galmisdale pier (NM 484 838)
Alternative finish	Cleadale war memorial (NM 477 887)
Time	6–7hr; 5–6hr to finish at Cleadale
Distance	17.8km (11 miles); 13.5km (8.4 miles) to finish at Cleadale
Total ascent	475m (1560ft); 425m (1395ft) to finish at Cleadale
Difficulty	This walk is hard going; it requires navigational care and route-finding across unpathed, rough ground, which can be pretty tiring
Terrain	Rough heathery ground, good grip on Beannan Breaca where pitchstone is exposed and tracks on approach/finish
Maps	OS Explorer 397; OS Landranger 39; Harvey Maps, Rùm, Eigg, Canna, Muck Superwalker XT25

While some minor navigation error is all it takes for this route to descend into a battle with eye-level tree branches, waist-deep heather and the prospect of precipitous, slippery crags, the reward for success is considerable. Despite a high point of only 312m, sprawling Beannan Breaca has a gloriously mountainous feel: a landscape of rocky knolls and miniature lochans with ever-changing views over the wild country of south-west Eigg, and beyond to Muck and Rùm. There's also a high probability that those intrepid enough to try, will be rewarded with having one-third of the island to themselves.

This hike does come with some warnings: despite not being exceptionally long, it's the hardest of those across the three smaller Small Isles, with no option for early abandonment, rough ground and a brief moment of easy, unexposed scrambling; beyond Grulin, long stretches are pathless and the short sections of sheep trails you do find are often leading in the wrong direction, so careful navigation is required – don't bother to attempt this route if visibility is poor.

From **Galmisdale pier**, follow the left-hand road fork leading north-west into woodland. After 500m go straight on – ignore the right-hand turning to the village hall and the left-hand turn shortly afterwards – climbing steadily until you

WALKING RÙM AND THE SMALL ISLES

reach a gate at the edge of the woods. Go through the gate and follow a track across a field towards a house, then pass through a gate on its right-hand side. Turn left onto a track and follow it west for 2km, until you reach the ruined settlement of **Grulin Uachdrach** (see Walk 13 for more information). From here, follow a path leading roughly north-west for a further 1.5km to reach **Grulin Iochdrach**.

Taking a break on the rocky, heathered slopes of Beannan Breaca

Continue north-west, following sheep paths, for about 800m, walking through a network of old field boundaries (marked on the 1:25,000 OS map). On reaching a grassy clearing (just east of an old field boundary on the west coast), turn right to head north-east, crossing the grassy clearing before heading east-north-east over difficult, heathery ground towards the steep slopes south-east of **Beannan Breaca**. Aim for the right-hand side (south) of a prominent, rounded, rocky hillock on the crest of the ridge, where a steep path follows the course of a small burn (not marked on the OS map) running down an obvious grassy clearing on the slope (NM 448 861).

Follow this path as it climbs with the burn initially on your left-hand side, until it becomes easier to cross it. At the top you should reach a semi-circular plateau sheltered by a theatre of steep crags. Walk south-east, following the base of these crags, for about 100m before scraps of a path indicate the easiest route to scramble up a short section of unexposed rock, bringing you to a high point level with two tiny lochans on your left (west), and a view over two larger, connected lochans on your right (south-east).

From here, no further scrambling is required as a path follows the rocky ridge-line north-west. The calm shores of Eigg's largest inland body of water, **Loch Beinn Tighe**, are soon visible on your right, while an uncommon view of An Sgùrr's northern face peaks over a skyline of pitchstone knolls to your rear.

In the north of **Beannan Breaca**'s lumpy summit plateau, there are **three small lochans**; follow the beginnings of a path heading north on the east side of the nearest (furthest east) of the three. The terrain then becomes tough going with close heather cover once again; but choose a good line of descent to avoid the steepest ground, while aiming for the base of the sheer western face of **Beinn Tighe**.

A landscape of rocky knolls, heather and lochans near the summit of Beannan Breaca

From beneath Beinn Tighe keep to higher ground heading north-east towards the western side of unassuming Sliabh Beinn Tighe (a minor hill just north-east of Beinn Tighe). There are impressive views of Rùm framed by the coastline on your left. Avoiding the summit, walk around the western edge of Sliabh Beinn Tighe to its northern slopes, before heading north-north-east towards a stream running through a gully with small willow trees growing beside it. The most obvious feature to aim towards here is a grassy clearing in the heather just beyond the gully, where you can make out the hint of a path leading up from the burn (NM 453 877).

After hopping over this small burn, walk across the clearing and – following sheep paths where possible – head north-north-east towards the cliffs above Poll Duchaill, where you will find a gate (NM 455 880). Go through the gate and head south-east along the clifftops for about 200m until you reach a burn. Cross this burn, and begin to descend north, then north-west, crossing the burn once more and heading down to a grassy area scattered with boulders below the cliffs at **Poll Duchaill**.

> If you aren't feeling too beaten down by the rugged nature of this walk, a short detour to a grassy promontory 150m north-west makes for a dramatic **picnic spot** with views of the plummeting coastline, sweeping bays of north-west Eigg, and out towards the Rùm Cuillin. Look out for cetaceans and basking sharks in the Sound of Rùm.

A distant Rùm from Poll Duchaill

To continue around the coast, head east, stepping over a lower section of the same stream you've crossed twice already, then keep to the higher ground above steep coastal slopes for about 500m as the elevation between yourself and the shoreline begins to decrease. Look out for an obvious path leading down to the shoreline on your left and take this opportunity to descend. Once you've reached lower ground, continue east on a grassy area just above the shore, until you come to a fence and gate leading into a field at **Laig**. To avoid crossing the mouth of a river at the southern end of Tràigh Chlithe, leave the shore to walk through the gate, and continue to follow the coastline on the inside of a stock fence until you reach another gate allowing you to cross a bridge.

Once over the bridge, head back to the shoreline on a track, which you can now follow north-east and then east – with another river on your left – all the way to the road. To shorten the walk by 4.8km and finish at **Cleadale**, turn left at the road and continue along it for 700m. For a circular walk, go right to walk along the quiet road to finish at **Galmisdale**; this takes just over an hour, taking you past Isle of Eigg Brewery, a 19th-century commemorative stone by the school, and views across the centre of the island as well as the sea on both sides.

WALK 16
The Beinn Bhuidhe plateau from Galmisdale

Start/finish	Galmisdale pier (NM 484 838)
Alternative finish	Cleadale war memorial (NM 477 887)
Time	7–8hr 30min; 5hr 30min–6hr 30min to finish at Cleadale
Distance	17.5km (10.9 miles); 12km (7.5 miles) to finish at Cleadale
Total ascent	430m (1410ft); 380m (1245ft) to finish at Cleadale
Difficulty	Rough ground covering the first half this route makes the walk pretty tough, though paths along the second half provide welcome relief
Terrain	Tracks, grassy fields, intermittent paths through dense heather cover on the east side of Beinn Bhuidhe and good paths on the west
Maps	OS Explorer 397; OS Landranger 39; Harvey Maps, Rùm, Eigg, Canna, Muck Superwalker XT25

Looking at the map, you'd be forgiven for assuming this route is fairly straightforward, but do not underestimate it – careful route finding (or obstinate determination) is required to follow intermittent paths through the dense heather and patchy bog above Beinn Bhuidhe's eastern cliffs. The compensation for your perseverance is an ever-changing perspective over the uninhabited north-east coastline and across the sound to Arisaig, Morar and Skye. Once past Dùnan Thalasgair, Beinn Bhuidhe's northernmost point, the second half of the walk is much less challenging: a well-defined path leads along the clifftops of Sgòrr an Fhàraidh and there are spectacular views across the sound to Rùm.

From **Galmisdale pier**, follow the road around the bay for 450m, turning right off the road to follow a track that continues round the bay. At the end of the track, cross a burn flowing out to the shore via stepping stones. Head north-east for about 250m across the greensward at Na Gurrabain and go through a metal gate. From here, bear left and follow a track north-west for about 60m before taking a right turn onto a faint, grassy path. Staying in the field some distance inland of the trees and low cliffs above Poll nam Partan, head north climbing gradually

Kildonan with Eilean Chathastail off the coast

across Na Breachnaich with a view of the small settlement at **Kildonan**. After about 600m, go through a metal gate some 200m west of the northern shore of **Poll nam Partan**. Continue to walk north, now following a track, for about 350m until you reach a gate to the road.

Turn right onto the road which leads down to Kildonan and follow it for 130m before turning left, crossing a wooden plank bridge onto a track road then passing a white house after 250m. A short detour south brings you to **St Donnán's Church** and burial ground.

This historic site appears to have been used for burials since prehistoric times and is also thought to be the site of Saint Donnán of Eigg's monastery, founded in the seventh century. The ruined **St Donnán's Church** that stands there now was built by the 16th-century MacDonald chiefs of Clanranald. Inside there are several interesting carvings including a stone slab with a double symmetrical cross inside a circle, thought to be from the eighth or ninth century; a small carving within a frame on the wall, which is said to be a pre-Christian female fertility carving or Sheela-na-gig (but could well be an 18th-century angel instead); and a number of early grave slabs. Outside the church there's an elaborate cross shaft dating from the late 14th century – its distinctive design is associated with the Iona school of sculpture.

Walk 16 – The Beinn Bhuidhe plateau from Galmisdale

At the white house, cross a burn, turn left onto a track and continue north-north-east. After 150m, the track splits – bear left, passing through a stock gate in a drystone wall.

Continue trending northwards along the track for 500m until it splits into multiple tractor tracks (and ends on the OS map); here you should head north, climbing for 300m to arrive at a fence. Turn right and walk along the fence, keeping it on your left.

Continue just past a sheepfold and head north to go through a gate in a stock fence. Bear right towards the clifftops, then head north keeping to a path with a fence between you and cliffs. Cross a burn running through a small canyon just below a small waterfall. Here the paths become less distinct, with dense heather and patches of sphagnum bog, but continue in the same direction for about 250m to another metal gate. Look out for white-tailed and golden eagles soaring around the cliffs here.

Go through the gate and continue along the clifftops following flattened paths through dense heather cover. While keeping the cliffs on your right is an invaluable navigational tool, no one path is easy to follow and caution is needed near the cliff edge, which is disguised by protruding heather in some places. The aerial perspective over a raised shore platform below **Beinn Bhuidhe**'s east cliffs – with the West Highland peaks laid out across the horizon – is a substantial reward for your efforts.

Trend slightly inland around Sgòrr Gobhar (to the east of An Cruachan) and continue north, crossing the occasional burn. After about 900m, be sure to take in the view where the Allt na h-Airde Mheadhonaich tumbles over the cliff edge. Just over 1km further on, by **Sròn na h-Iolaire**, leave the cliff edge as it begins to lose height – keep your height and contour along, trending north-west. There are vague paths to aid your progress and the heather cover is less dense. Cross the Allt Ceann a' Gharaid, which flows out from Loch na Beinne Bhuidhe, continue north-west and you will soon arrive at the cliff edge once more. Follow the clifftop north-west to **Dùnan Thalasgair** where there are fine views of the Skye Cuillin in clear conditions.

From the north-west end of Dùnan Thalasgair, turn south-east and follow a fence for a short distance to a gate; go through the gate and follow the path outside the fence along the clifftops for a short way. The views of Rùm are unbeatable on a clear day. Turn around the end of the fence and continue south along the narrow but distinct path along the clifftops, soon passing a 'Vanessa' **triangulation pillar** at 336m, some 50m east of the cliff edge.

Continue along the soft, springy turf on the clifftop path, enjoying magnificent views of the layered basalt cliffs further south, and passing over the high point of **Sgòrr an Fhàraidh** after a further 1km. The path begins to descend steadily

Following the clifftop path along north-east Beinn Bhuidhe

along the cliff edge and arrives above the impressive waterfall of the **Allt Bidein an Tighearna** after another 1km. Cross the burn and enjoy the view from behind the rock pinnacle known as Bidein an Tighearna – the 'Finger of God' – down across Cleadale and the Bay of Laig. Continue to descend south-west for around 350m from Allt Bidein an Tighearna, following the clifftops on the obvious path until you reach a step stile on your right.

Cross the step stile over a fence and turn left for a short distance before bearing right and following the path running into a gully and over a dip in an old stone wall. Follow the path as it descends, taking the less steep option to the right, then cross a wooden stile over a fence before finally emerging under Lageorna bed and breakfast's washing line.

To shorten the walk and finish at **Cleadale**'s war memorial junction, turn right and walk a short distance. For **Galmisdale**, turn left and follow the road south for 5.5km.

WALK 17
Sgorr an Fhàraidh

Start/finish	Cleadale war memorial (NM 477 887)
Time	1hr 30min–2hr 30min
Distance	6.3km (3.9 miles)
Total ascent	305m (1000ft)
Difficulty	Apart from a steep ascent, this route is fairly straightforward and navigationally unchallenging
Terrain	Springy moorland paths above Sgorr an Fhàraidh and grassy fields with a short steep section of ascent
Maps	OS Explorer 397; OS Landranger 39; Harvey Maps, Rùm, Eigg, Canna, Muck Superwalker XT25

With half the route following airy clifftops and the remainder meandering along a single-track road and paths below, there are no dull moments on this short but spectacular walk. Following the natural curve of Sgorr an Fhàraidh creates an ever-changing perspective on the cliffs' dramatic landslip formations and towering layers of volcanic rock, while northern Eigg's scattered settlements are laid out like a map a few hundred metres below. Beyond the sandy beaches of the north-west coast, the mountainous outline of neighbouring Rùm also holds your attention for most of the route. This walk is best avoided in strong winds, but otherwise presents no real difficulties beyond an initial steep ascent.

From the war memorial junction in **Cleadale**, follow the road south for a short distance until you've just passed the timber-clad Lageorna bed and breakfast. Turn left then walk under the washing line and follow a path up to a wooden stile. Cross the stile and continue to follow the path as it climbs towards a steep gully between two distinct rock stacks jutting from the cliff (the right-hand one being particularly sharp). Walk up through this gully, crossing a low point in a drystane dike. On emerging from the gully, bear left and continue following a path climbing to a wooden step stile.

Cross the stile and turn left, walking initially north-eastwards following a well-trodden path along the clifftops; soon you will the pass Bidein an Tighearna or the Finger of God, a distinctive rock pinnacle projecting from the cliff. Cross

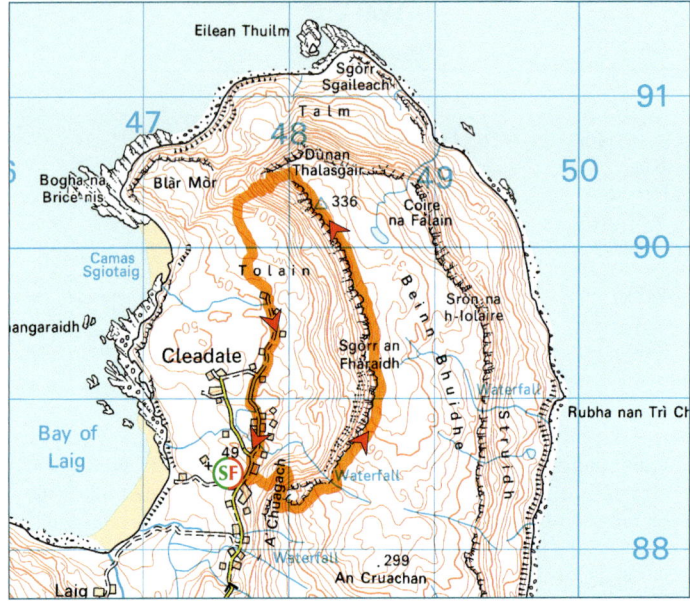

the Allt Bidein an Tighearna burn and continue along the path, which follows the line of the clifftops. The concave curve of Sgorr an Fhàraidh presents spectacular views of its sheer basalt cliffs and frames the bird's-eye views over Cleadale and the Bay of Laig, Howlin, Tolain and Camas Sgiotaig (Walk 18). Beyond Eigg's west coast, the Rùm Cuillin dominate the horizon. This is also a great vantage point for spotting golden eagles.

After about 1km, continue over the unmarked summit of **Sgorr an Fhàraidh** (340m) and a further 1km will bring you to some small tarns and a 'Vanessa' **triangulation pillar** (50m east of the cliff edge). A little further north, a fence begins beside the cliffs. Taking care to stay away from the edge, there's a path and adequate space to continue following the clifftops with the fence on the right-hand (landward) side. Some 20m south-east of a final crown of rock at **Dùnan Thalasgair** (a worthwhile detour for panoramic views), the beginnings of a path lead downhill on your left (west). Follow the path as it descends a series of zigzags. Look out for light purple heath spotted orchids growing among the grass in spring and summer.

Sgorr an Fhàraidh with a distant An Sgùrr

At the bottom of the descent, just before you reach a fence, turn left onto a path leading south towards the red-roofed barn and stone-walled enclosures at Five Pennies. From here, turn right onto a track leading south to Tolain, Howlin and ultimately back to **Cleadale**.

In 2002, Eigg historian Camille Dressler was reported in *The Herald* as saying, 'I have no way of proving it, but there has been a long-standing local story that **Tolkien** stayed in it [the house at Howlin] in the 1930s or 1940s and that the views of Rùm had inspired him in writing *Lord of the Rings*.'

WALK 18
Camas Sgiotaig and the north-west coast

Start/finish	Cleadale war memorial (NM 477 887)
Time	1hr 30min–2hr
Distance	6km (3.7 miles)
Total ascent	160m (525ft)
Difficulty	This route is not too difficult, but a little navigation is required and some care is needed over coastal rocks
Terrain	Tracks, grassy fields, sandy beach and rocky shoreline
Maps	OS Explorer 397; OS Landranger 39; Harvey Maps, Rùm, Eigg, Canna, Muck Superwalker XT25

This rewarding short route is a minor coastal adventure, starting with Eigg's most secluded stretch of sand, Camas Sgiotaig, before clambering around a shoreline of weather and sea-sculpted sandstone formations between the outreaching skerries of Bogha na Brice-nis and the layered cliffs of Blàr Mòr. The mighty Rùm Cuillin dominate the horizon throughout, until the final ascent to the saddle between Dùnan Thalasgair and Guala Mhòr (Blàr Mòr) gives a spectacular view across the sound to Skye.

At the war memorial junction in **Cleadale**, take the left-hand fork and follow the road for around 600m until it peters out by a house and some farm buildings. Where a wooden signpost indicates 'Singing Sands', follow the track, passing through a gate as it swings left to the rear of the house then continues intermittently north-westwards across fields, crossing an old drystone wall, to the edge of low cliffs. Turn right and continue north along the cliff edge inside a stock fence, then cross a stile on your left to descend to the beach (a second stile to cross just above the shore is usually decorated with washed-up plastic debris). The 'singing sands' of Camas Sgiotaig are formed by eroded round quartzite grains, which make a distinctive squeak when scuffed underfoot.

Take some time to explore the beach, with its spotless sands fringed by weird and wonderful weathered sandstone sculptures, before walking along to the north end of Tràigh na Bìgil. Cross rocks and pebbles to continue north-west and then north-east around the coast, just above the shore on a narrow, trodden path,

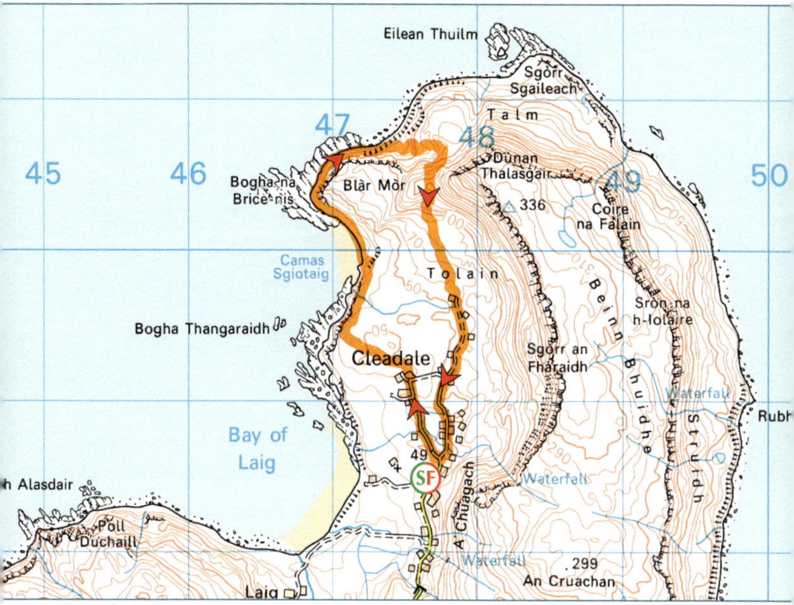

WALK 18 – CAMAS SGIOTAIG AND THE NORTH-WEST COAST

The final stile to Camas Sgiotaig is often adorned with collected ocean plastic

The Rùm Cuillin from Camas Sgiotaig

which is a little awkward to follow in places. Across the Sound of Rùm, the bothy at Dibidil is only 6.5km away and is sometimes visible in certain light conditions, while the mountainous Cuillin seem within touching distance.

Between the skerries of **Bogha na Brice-nis** and the sedimentary layers of Blàr Mòr's cliffs, huge spherical concretions of Jurassic sedimentary rock form boulders of cemented sandstone reminiscent of giant, cracked dragon eggs.

After 800m you'll see the imposing sharpened peak of Dùnan Thalasgair, the northern tip of the Beinn Bhuidhe plateau. Head to its base, climbing up across boulder-strewn Bealach Thuilm on a network of sheep paths (bracken makes this trickier in summer) and find an obvious diagonal path heading up between Dùnan Thalasgair and Guala Mhòr (Blàr Mòr). Follow this path up to the saddle, and as you begin to descend, head to and over small stile in a stock fence. Cross the stile and follow an intermittent grassy path to a red-roofed barn and stone-walled enclosures at Five Pennies (a ruined township just north of Howlin, between Cleadale and Tolain), where you can pick up the track heading south back to **Cleadale**.

WALK 19
Around the north-east coast of Eigg

Start/finish	Cleadale war memorial (NM 477 887)
Time	6–7hr
Distance	14.8km (9.2 miles)
Total ascent	500m (1640ft)
Difficulty	Varied terrain, some without obvious paths, can make this route a bit challenging at times; it's harder in summer when bracken and other vegetation is at its highest
Terrain	Grassy coastal paths and indistinct paths through heather moorland
Maps	OS Explorer 397; OS Landranger 39; Harvey Maps, Rùm, Eigg, Canna, Muck Superwalker XT25

This glorious coastal route visits Talm at Eigg's most northerly point, before heading south along a raised shore platform below the island's dramatic eastern cliffs. With walls of towering basalt to landward, and views across the sound to Sleat, Morar and Arisaig, the scenery alone is ample reward, but this remote part of Eigg is also a great place to spot golden or white-tailed eagles, harbour porpoises and other cetaceans.

Route finding presents no difficulties until the final stretch up and over the Beinn Bhuidhe plateau, where rough terrain with close heather cover and soggy patches of sphagnum bog makes for tough going in places. Any hardship is easily outweighed by dramatic views from both east and west clifftops, and from An Cruachan, which gives a unique vantage point over the south of Eigg.

At the war memorial junction in **Cleadale**, take the right-hand fork and continue along the road passing the settlement's scattering of houses. The road soon becomes a track as it passes through Howlin heading towards Tolain. About 1km from the war memorial, as you pass some old stone-built livestock pens and a red-roofed barn, bear left, leaving the track, and continue along a path, passing the ruins of Five Pennies.

> The name **Five Pennies** refers to 'pennylands', part of a Norse system for valuing land according to the quality of the soil. The survival of this agricultural

WALKING RÙM AND THE SMALL ISLES

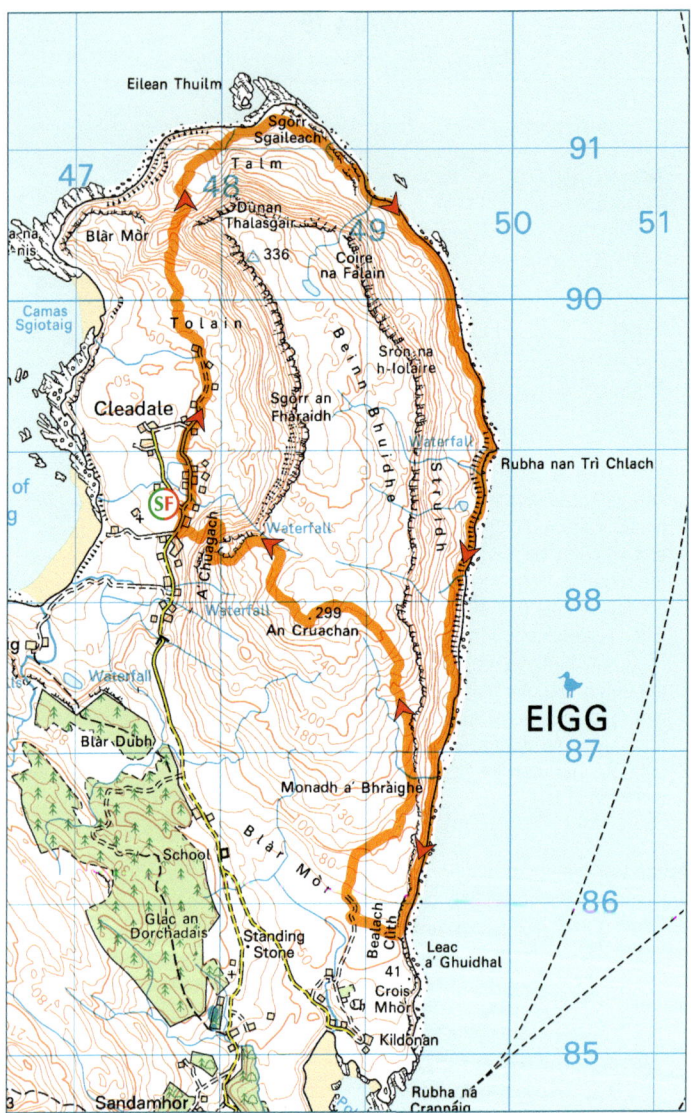

Walk 19 – Around the north-east coast of Eigg

place name gives strength to the argument of Norse settlement here, rather than just passing Viking raids.

While the rough, grassy path is unclear at times and prone to bogginess, follow as it climbs north steadily up towards the saddle between Guala Mhòr and **Dùnan Thalasgair**, crossing a stock fence by a step stile some 100m from the highest point.

To descend from the saddle, bear right following a path that's initially distinct as it loses height beneath the north-west flank of the cliffs immediately below Dùnan Thalasgair. Where the path levels amid a terrain of scattered rocks, follow it round to the north-east, making for a broad gully. Cross to the eastern side of the gully and follow it past a ruined house down to the shore next to an old drystone-walled enclosure at **Talm**. The scant remains of around 20 stone buildings at Talm were once used for summer shielings. Seals can usually be seen basking on Eilean Thuilm a few hundred metres offshore, with both Rùm and Skye Cuillin on the horizon.

Continue initially east following a narrow path to the landward side of the low cliff at **Sgòrr Sgaileach**. Climb a little over Fhaing Ruadh and then descend to the shore following a small gully a short way before skirting around to the left briefly to find the easiest line down to a pebble beach.

Descending to the coast at Talm

Walk south-east a short way along the edge of the pebble beach and then continue along a narrow path. High above, the impressive waterfall of the Allt Ceann a' Gharaid drops precipitously over the distant cliff edge. Stay with this path along the raised shore platform for the next 5km, with east Beinn Bhuidhe's magnificent basalt cliffs on your right and uninterrupted views of Sleat, Morar and Arisaig across the water.

The steep cliffs around **Beinn Bhuidhe** were formed 60 million years ago by vast flood-basalt lava flows. Iron-rich layers of soil, which formed during breaks in volcanic activity, subsequently eroded faster than the lava flows themselves, forming the distinctive step-like profile visible today.

The path is generally easy to follow and stays just above the shore for the most part, until the final 1km where it begins to climb as the gradient between the shore and the foot of the cliffs steepens approaching Bealach Clìth. The path becomes more distinct at this point and is even marked on the 1:25,000 OS map. The going can be awkward at times with rough ground and rocks to negotiate in places, along with patches of chest-high bracken to battle in summer.

The saddle between Guala Mhòr and Dùnan Thalasgair can serve as a wind tunnel

Beinn Bhuidhe's basalt cliffs tower over the east coast

Follow the path up through the gap in the cliffs by the **Bealach Clìth**, climb to a metal gate and go through.

To return to Cleadale via the summit of An Cruachan, continue west-north-west over waterlogged ground along the course of an old drystone wall for 300m, then turn right (north) onto a track. After 50m bear left, ignoring a less obvious track leading east, and continue for a further 130m until the track ends on the OS map and splits into numerous tractor tracks; here you should head north, climbing, for about 300m to arrive at a fence. Turn right and walk along the fence keeping it on your left.

Continue just past a stone-built sheepfold and walk 80m north to go through a gate in a stock fence. Follow a grassy path bearing right towards the clifftops, then head north keeping to a path with a fence between you and clifftops across increasingly rough ground. Cross a burn running through a small canyon just below a tiny waterfall. Here the paths become less distinct, with dense heather and boggy areas, but continue in the same direction for about 250m to another metal gate.

Go through the gate and continue near the clifftops for another 100m to reach the top of a slender waterfall (NM 493 872). From here, bear left (inland) and follow vague paths through the dense heather cover to climb roughly north-north-west then north-west for about 1km to gain the summit of **An Cruachan** (299m), marked with a small stone-pile cairn. This marginally elevated position over the otherwise fairly featureless moorland landscape of central Beinn Bhuidhe provides great views across the south of Eigg.

From the summit, head north-west, descending steadily for about 350m, before picking up a vague path heading north towards Allt Bidein an Tighearna for a further 280m. Follow the southern bank of this small burn north-west until it reaches the south-western cliffs of the Beinn Bhuidhe plateau, where it cascades off the clifftop. There are dramatic views out over the sands of Laig Bay to the Rùm Cuillin across the Sound of Rùm.

Turn left and walk south-west a short distance to Bidein an Tighearna ('God's Finger'), taking a moment to admire this distinctively shaped rock pinnacle, before continuing along the clifftop along the obvious path for around 350m, until you reach a step stile (NM 480 883) on your right.

Cross the stile and then turn left. Follow a path south-west for about 50m before bearing right as a path leads into a gully and over a dip in an old stone wall. Follow this path as it descends, taking a right where the option of a more gradual descent is offered, crossing a stile over a fence and eventually coming out under Lageorna bed and breakfast's washing line. Turn right along the road for 160m to return to the start at the war memorial junction in **Cleadale**.

CANNA AND SANDAY

Cliffs above the east coast of Canna (Walk 21)

Canna Harbour from Sanday (Walk 22)

CANNA AND SANDAY

Canna is the westernmost and second smallest of the Small Isles archipelago. It is linked to its tide-separated sibling, Sanday, by a bridge as well as sandbanks at low tide. Canna is approximately 8km long and 1.5km wide, while Sanday is about 1.5km long and 0.5km wide – the residents of both islands consider themselves a single community.

The bulk of Canna rises up to two plateaux 50–200m above sea level, which are joined by a low-lying isthmus at Tarbert. The dramatic coastline, with its remarkable geological features, spectacular scenery and ancient monuments, provides the main focus for walkers. Towering basalt cliffs rise above the north and south-west coasts, with the island's highest point – Carn a' Ghaill (210m) – in the north-east; the gentler south coast has a series of small beaches. The entire island can be walked round in one long day or split into two more manageable chunks. Sanday can be strolled around in a few hours and is well worth a visit, particularly to watch the puffins nesting on the sea stacks of Dùn Mòr and Dùn Beag from April to July. In fine weather, the smaller island's south coast has glorious views over to the north-west of Rùm.

There is a large natural harbour between Canna and Sanday with a substantial pier, used by the Caledonian MacBrayne ferry, *MV Lochnevis*, which connects Canna and the neighbouring Small Isles with the mainland port of Mallaig. The sheltered, deep-water harbour is the only one of its type in the Small Isles, and attracts considerable yachting traffic.

In 1981, Canna and Sanday were given to the National Trust for Scotland (NTS) by their previous owners, the Gaelic folklorists and scholars John Lorne Campbell and Margaret Fay Shaw. The islands are now primarily run as a farm and conservation area, with some crofting on Sanday. The Canna community and the NTS are working to improve facilities for residents and visitors, including a new Visitor Hub by the pier, and the restoration or repurposing of historic buildings; at the time of this book's publication, work is ongoing in Canna House, while it's only just begun at Coroghon Barn by Black Sand Beach.

The island has tracks, but no surfaced roads.

GEOLOGY

Canna and Sanday are largely composed of lavas erupted during the Lower Tertiary Period from a major volcano on what would become the Isle of Skye. While the volcano was erupting, the area was traversed by fast-flowing rivers which deposited thick layers of boulder conglomerate. These boulders were rounded as they were carried along in the immensely powerful rapid-flowing currents – the largest are over a metre in diameter.

Canna is also noted for the tiers of basalt pillars rising over the eastern half of the island and the sea cliffs that dominate its northern shore. On the eastern edge of the island, Compass Hill (139m) is formed of volcanic rock known as tuff, which is of such high iron content that passing ships' compasses are distorted, pointing east, rather than north. Raised shore platforms occur, notably beneath the cliffs in the island's west. Along the coastline near the south-eastern extremity of Sanday stand two impressive sea stacks, Dùn Mòr and Dùn Beag, which are formed of columnar basalt lavas and boulder conglomerate.

The dramatic high cliffs beneath Beinn Tighe (Walk 21)

HISTORY

Canna has been inhabited for at least 5000 years, with extensive finds of Neolithic pottery made at Tarbert. A fortification known as Dùn Channa, possibly dating to the Bronze Age, sits atop a rock stack at the island's western extremity. By around 600CE, Canna was likely occupied by a mixture of Celtic and pre-Celtic peoples generally described as Picts.

The earliest historical references relate to the patron saint of the island, Saint Columba (521–597CE), after whom two of the churches are named. There are traces of two early Christian sites on the island: at A' Chill, where a stone cross dates from the eighth century; and at Sgorr nam Bànnaomha (Cliff of the Holy Women), a walled enclosure situated on a raised shore platform below steep cliffs that is thought to have been a nunnery.

Like the rest of the Hebrides, Canna was affected by Viking raids and subsequent settlement from the ninth century. The Norse influence is evident in the place names 'Sanday' and 'Tarbert' and also the site known as Uamh Rìgh Lochlainn, the Cave of the Norse King, which is believed to be a burial site, although there is no archaeological evidence to support this. If monastic life on Canna was disrupted by Viking raids, it had resumed by the early 13th and continued until at least the 15th century with the island remaining the property of Iona Abbey until 1627.

With the end of Norse rule in the 12th century, Canna became part of the territory of the MacDonalds of Clanranald – the Lords of the Isles. Under Clanranald rule, the island's population found itself involved in the MacDonald clan's feuds and rebellions against the Crown. In 1588, Canna – along with the other Small Isles – was laid waste by Lachlan Maclean of Duart leading a raiding party of a hundred Spanish marines from a galleon of the defeated Armada anchored at Tobermory. The islands' settlements were razed and their inhabitants murdered.

In 1745, Canna men were among those enlisted with Bonnie Prince Charlie's forces during the second Jacobite rising. In the wake of the failed rebellion, harsh reprisals were visited on the islanders by government troops.

The failure of the rising undermined Clanranald's fortunes and, by the early 19th century – when the kelp market collapsed and made Canna unprofitable – the clan was deeply in debt. Clanranald was obliged to sell most of its territories, including Canna at a point when the island's population had peaked at over 400.

The new lairds, Donald MacNeil and his son, found the Canna community to be a bad investment, and a series of Clearances saw most residents moved to poorer land on Sanday. A' Chill, situated at the head of the natural harbour, was Canna's main settlement until its residents were evicted in the mid-19th century. The post-Clearance population of Canna and Sanday was recorded as 119 in 1881, but it continued to decline, stabilising at around 20 during the second half of the 20th century.

Canna was bought by Dr John Lorne Campbell, the eminent Gaelic scholar and author, in 1938. He widened the pier, improved the soil, increased the amount of woodland and modernised the cottages of his crofting tenants. He also farmed the land himself, rearing sheep and cattle. Campbell and his wife, the American musician Margaret Fay Shaw, travelled throughout the Hebrides

A Marian shrine near the bridge between Canna and Sanday (Walk 22)

Puffins around Dùn Mòr (Walk 22)

collecting Gaelic folklore and songs: their archive is kept at Canna House, their former home, and was given to the NTS along with the islands. At the 2001 census, the population had dwindled to 12, but new residents have since settled, bringing it back up to around 20.

Today, most of the island is managed by the NTS as a single livestock farm. Farming is an important part of Canna's economy, and the island supports around 600 Cheviot ewes and 50 cows as well as a small fold of Highland cattle. Conservation of the island's landscape, monuments and habitats, together with the encouragement of rare species – including the corncrake and white-tailed eagle – are high on the agenda. Sanday is still crofted by some of its inhabitants.

WILDLIFE

Aside from livestock, there are no large land mammals on Canna, but there are otters. By 2005 the island's brown rat population had grown to 10,000, posing such a threat to nesting birds, including the rare Manx shearwater, that a complete cull was necessary. As rodenticide was used, a breeding population of the island's distinct race of woodmice, *Apodemus sylvaticus*, was removed beforehand. By the end of 2006 Canna was declared rat-free. The mice were returned and are thriving. However, since the eradication of the rats the rabbit population has grown exponentially causing erosion to the clifftops. White-tailed eagles, golden eagles and buzzards will take rabbits, but they have their work cut out. Hedgehogs were introduced in 1938.

Canna is renowned for its birdlife, including white-tailed eagles, golden eagles, peregrine falcons, buzzards, hooded crows, ravens and the elusive corncrake. Seabirds breeding on the island include puffins, guillemots, kittiwakes, fulmars and the great skua or 'bonxie'. Predation by rats seriously affected Canna's seabird colonies, particularly razorbills, shags and Manx shearwaters, but these are recovering well since the rat eradication programme. In the surrounding waters, Atlantic grey and common seals, dolphins, porpoises, minke whales and basking sharks can be seen.

There are many varieties of butterflies and moths, some of which are rare. Butterfly species include green hairstreak, speckled wood, grayling, small pearl-bordered fritillary and dark green fritillary. Moths include death's-head hawkmoth, sallow kitten, yellow horned, pale oak eggar, white ermine, dew moth, nut-tree tussock, large emerald, transparent burnet, ghost moth and bee moth.

WOODLAND, PLANTS AND FLOWERS

There is little indigenous woodland on Canna – a few specimens of rowan, hazel, aspen, sallow and creeping willow are all that remain. Much of the native tree cover was probably felled for firewood when the island was more populous, and the introduction of sheep and rabbits inhibited regeneration. A number of species have been introduced – mostly since 1881 – including sycamore, wych elm, cherry, hawthorn, ash, elder, lime, whitebeam and Serbian spruce. Exotics include Antarctic beech, southern beech and dawn redwood.

The island's mild, Gulf Stream-assisted climate, fertile soil and sheltered position have earned Canna the name 'garden of the Hebrides'. Among the island's many plant species, bell heather, lady fern and various grasses, sedges, rushes, thistles and umbellifers thrive amid the varied terrain. Sea pinks grow along the shore, daffodils proliferate in March and April, bluebells and flag iris abound in spring and primroses can be found almost year-round. Canna has several varieties of orchid: marsh spotted, heath spotted, early purple, frog and the rare greater butterfly orchid.

GETTING AROUND

Visitors are not permitted to bring vehicles, and there is no public transport on the island's few kilometres of track road. Getting around on foot or by bike are the only options, but luggage transfer is usually offered with accommodation.

AMENITIES

The Isle of Canna's website (www.theisleofcanna.com) lists amenities,

On the north side of Canna's narrow waist (Walk 21)

accommodation and other up-to-date information about the island.

The unstaffed Canna community shop is open around the clock and operates on an honesty system (payment via cash or card). The shop stocks a range of groceries and essentials as well as souvenirs; however, it's still advisable to bring some supplies with you. The building also has free drinking water and Wi-Fi, plus an inexpensive hot drinks facility. The post office is located in a green shed next to a telephone box, close to The Square. Phone signal is best on O2. Toilets for public use can be found at the pier and community shop. Shelter is available at the farm steading with tables and chairs, heaters and facilities for making hot drinks. A new Visitor Hub at the pier, opened for the 2025 season, provides toilets, showers and laundry facilities, as well as an office for the NTS Canna Ranger.

Café Canna (tel 016187 482488 www.cafecanna.co.uk), the island's licensed café and restaurant, is open from mid-April to late September, serving brunch, lunch and dinner (check online for opening hours). Specialities include locally sourced seafood and game. Vegetarian options are also available and there is a well-stocked bar.

PLACES TO STAY

Canna Campsite (off-site tel 01687 462963 www.cannacampsite.com) has tent pitches and three camping pods (sleeping two–four) at the campsite, as well as two caravans (each sleeping four), a cabin and a bunkhouse. The campsite, which is situated in a peaceful spot above the village, has running water, toilets, showers, a cooking shack, picnic benches and a campfire area. The bunkhouse is a traditional white-washed stone cottage (sleeps eight), situated beneath columnar basalt cliffs on the hillside above A' Chill. It has a kitchen, bunkbeds, a toilet, shower and a wood-burning stove as well as tremendous views across Canna Harbour to Sanday and Rùm beyond. Across the bridge from the campsite, the self-catering Sanday Cabin (sleeps two; minimum two-night stay) provides a more upmarket option with en suite toilet/shower room and kitchen. Bedding is provided for Sanday Cabin and the caravans, and can be hired for the other accommodation.

Tighard Guesthouse (tel 01687 462474 www.tighard-isleofcanna.com) has three spacious bedrooms in a fine Edwardian house with a spectacular outlook situated above the harbour. Breakfast is included, while dinner and packed lunches are available on request.

Canna Self Catering (www.canna-selfcatering.co.uk) has three cottages situated on Sanday (sleeping four–six) with all the usual amenities.

Canna Bunkhouse

WALK 20
A' Chill, Compass Hill and Black Sand Beach

Start/finish	Canna community shop (NG 275 055)
Time	1–2hr
Distance	4km (2.5 miles)
Total ascent	125m (410ft)
Difficulty	An easy walk if care is taken to follow navigational instructions
Terrain	Grassy and heathery paths
Maps	OS Explorer 397; OS Landranger 39; Harvey Maps, Rùm, Eigg, Canna, Muck Superwalker XT25

This short circular route transcends expectations with magnificent views over Sanday, Rùm and the Skye Cuillin sandwiched between the unique archaeological sites at A' Chill and Coroghon Castle. The walk finishes at Black Sand Beach, one of Canna's most beautiful stretches of sand and a perfect spot for a picnic.

From Canna community shop, follow the track south-west for 500m until you reach St Columba's Chapel. Follow signs for 'A' Chill' and 'Celtic Cross' and go through a gate on your right, between St Columba's Chapel and the adjacent farm buildings, and follow a grassy path beside a drystone wall for 100m. Approach a fenced area of woodland, bear right and head north between a rocky knoll and the fence towards a gate, marked with an orange arrow in its furthest west corner.

Go through the gate and walk roughly north along a meandering woodland path through broad-leafed trees for 200m, until you reach a small gate. A carpet of bluebells covers the woodland floor in springtime.

Go through the gate and turn left (west), passing through a second gate – the sculptured Celtic cross and standing Punishment Stone at **A' Chill** are a short distance beyond.

From the Punishment Stone descend a short distance to a fence on its west side, then turn right (north) and walk along the fence until you reach a gate on your left. Go through this, turn right and head north across a grassy field towards a gate in a drystone wall.

WALK 20 – A' CHILL, COMPASS HILL AND BLACK SAND BEACH

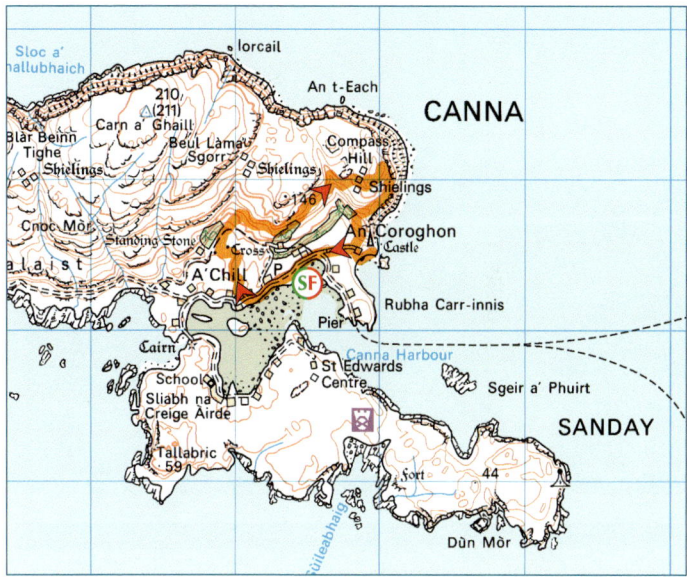

Go through the gate onto an initially muddy, then grassy track leading north-eastwards uphill. After 130m, as the track turns right running below the line of a fence, leave it and instead go through a gate in a stock fence on your left. A muddy path leads uphill straight ahead; follow this briefly before turning right where a less obvious path crosses a small burn and contours east around the south side of a low hill. The view over Sanday towards Rùm is already quite spectacular and only becomes more dramatic as you climb towards Compass Hill.

Pass two large, rectangular water tanks on your right and follow the path as it begins to trend north-east below basalt crags. Rise above the copse of trees that surrounds Tighard Guesthouse and continue along the path through bracken and boulders, staying on the landward side of a fence on your right.

When the far end of this fence reaches a junction, there is a [currently very decrepit] wooden gate. Pass through this gate as best as you can; Compass Hill is directly ahead. Follow grassy paths as they head straight, before veering left to contour around the head of the valley between Blàr na Carraigh and Cnoc na Carraigh, avoiding the worst of the height loss. Continue up to **Compass Hill** and around the south side of its western flank, where the hint of a steep grassy path leads up between two basalt crags to its summit. Compass Hill is formed of

A' Chill's weathered Celtic cross

A' CHILL

The 32 houses that once comprised A' Chill were flattened after residents were evicted in 1851 to make way for sheep; the settlement's graveyard is all that remains. An impressive eighth- or ninth-century cross has outlasted the village, depicting the *Adoration of the Magi*, where the 'three kings' gave baby Jesus gifts, and various animals. Standing slightly higher, the Punishment Stone is said to have been used as an ancient form of corporal punishment where the offender's thumb was jammed into a small hole.

a volcanic rock known as tuff, which has such a high iron content that passing ships' compasses are distorted, pointing east rather than north.

Walk to the far east end of Compass Hill, where there are great views of the Skye Cuillin to the north-east, as well as Rùm and Sanday to the south-east. Follow a path down to a fence running along the top of the eastern sea cliffs; turn right here and head downhill (south). Follow a path alongside the fence, staying on its landward side until it meets a drystone wall, which you can then follow down to a gate.

Go through the gate, turn left and walk downhill, directly across the middle of a grassy field to another gate just right and in front of a dilapidated stone building at **An Coroghon**.

Compass Hill behind An Coroghon and Black Sand Beach

Go through the gate and walk towards the sea, passing through a second gate onto the strikingly variegated Black Sand Beach. Unless the tide is very high, you can wander around to the left for a closer look at **Coroghon Castle**.

The small stone structure known as **Coroghon Castle** clings to the basalt stack of Coroghon Mòr, some 20m above the ground. The ruin consists of two rooms incorporating the natural rock as partial walls. It's thought to have been a prison, used in the 17th century for the clearly unbalanced Donald MacDonald of Clanranald to hold his wife, Marion MacLeod, hostage. Visitors are asked not to climb inside to prevent further damage to the unstable ruin, as well as for their own safety.

To return to **Canna Harbour** and the shop, go back through the same gate above the beach, walk a short distance and then turn left onto a substantial track – you can follow this back to the village.

WALK 21
Around Canna

Start/finish	Canna community shop (NG 275 055)
Time	7–9hr; east Canna only 3hr 30min–4hr 30min; west Canna only 5–6hr 30min
Distance	20km (12.4 miles); east Canna only 10.3km (6.4 miles); west Canna only 18km (11.2 miles)
Total ascent	605m (1985ft); east Canna only 275m (900ft); west Canna only 445m (1460ft)
Difficulty	One very long day or a couple of shorter ones, this route is tough if tackled as a whole; the south coast makes for easier walking than the north, but both sections of this walk include some of each coast
Terrain	Intermittent paths through rough heathery ground, grassy slopes and track
Maps	OS Explorer 397; OS Landranger 39; Harvey Maps, Rùm, Eigg, Canna, Muck Superwalker XT25

While this fine circular route around Canna's magnificent coastline is exposed to the elements for much of its course, the island's dramatic high cliffs provide fantastic views of Skye, Rùm, Barra and South Uist on a clear day. Additionally, there are several sites of historical interest along the route, and the island's high point, Carn a' Ghaill (210m), is close to the clifftop path. The terrain is not especially tough and, though there can be patches of bog, the heather is kept short by the wind and narrow paths can be found along much of the clifftops. A track running along the raised shore platform between Canna Harbour and Tarbert provides a convenient way to split this demanding day walk into two parts, east and west. To walk just west Canna, start the instructions from subheading 'West Canna only'.

From Canna community shop walk east-north-east along the road, soon taking the left-hand fork along a track where the road bears south-east towards the pier. Continue along the track towards the rock stack of Coroghon Mòr (Walk 20), with its crumbling stone turret. Before reaching Coroghon Mòr there is a junction in the track just before a ruined stone building at **An Coroghon**; here, go through a

The path above the towering north-eastern cliffs with Iorcail sea stack offshore

metal gate in a drystone wall on your left, and walk north, uphill, across a field towards another metal gate in a wall on the opposite side of the field. Go through the gate and turn right.

Follow a grassy track, then a path as it climbs along the line of a wall which gives way to a fence running above the clifftops. Take a short detour to the summit of **Compass Hill** (139m), the high point at Canna's eastern end, before heading back to the clifftops and continuing north following a small path above the precipitous eastern cliffs.

On a clear day, the panoramic views from **Compass Hill** make a detour to its summit worthwhile: to the north and north-east Skye dominates the horizon, with Glenbrittle and the Black Cuillin just across the sound, while looking south-east, low-lying Sanday provides an idyllic foreground to the imposing western hills of Rùm.

From the north-east corner of the clifftops continue west following a narrow path winding its course a little way back from the cliff edge – there are sections of stock fence along the clifftops at strategic points. North-west of Cnoc na Carraigh, cross a stock fence via a step stile (NG 275 063), and head north-west along a narrow clifftop path through low heather cover. An impressive natural arch juts out from the rocky coastline below, while the monolith sea stack, Iorcail stands slightly offshore to the north-west.

After 600m, you will arrive at a section of fence with a broken stile crossing to the clifftops above a steep-sided geo; ignore this and continue inside the fence, following an obvious path, before it descends a short way to cross a burn. Continue along the clifftop, soon crossing the 200m contour on the northern side of **Carn a' Ghaill** (210m); a 150m detour south takes you to Canna's highest point, marked with a 'Vanessa' **triangulation pillar**. In late spring and early summer, ethereal cotton grass blows hypnotically in the wind on the gentle slopes of Carn a' Ghaill.

Continue along the narrow clifftop path, losing a little height. Stay on the inside of the fence where a trio of gullies tumble precipitously down to the shore at **Sloc a' Ghallubhaich** – there is a dramatic view north-west along the sea cliffs beneath Beinn Tighe. Walk on, climbing a short way to cross a fence by a step stile, then continue up and over the seaward flank of **Beinn Tighe**. Continue near the cliffs along the flank of the hill before dropping north-west on a steep, grassy zigzag path on the inside of a fence as the barn at Tarbert comes into view.

Cross a broad gully, which is boggy in places, then follow a vague path just above the clifftop fence line, with low rocky crags on your left, as you rise again over Buidhe Sgòrr. When the fence runs out, keep to paths some way back from the edge (some of the more precipitous options end dramatically by plunging over the edge). There are glorious views over the outreaching Rubha Langanes headland below.

From the western flank of Buidhe Sgòrr, leave the clifftops and head south for just over 100m until you reach a low drystone wall. Cross the wall and continue a further 120m south, walking across a grassy mound to visit the twin entrances to an Iron Age **souterrain** (NG 244 063).

This is the only example of a souterrain in the Small Isles. Predominantly underground structures, **souterrains** are thought to have been used for storage rather than dwelling, possibly as places to keep grain. The two visible entrances to Canna's souterrain are modern breaks, which provide access through the roof into a passageway.

Turn right and walk south-west, crossing the drystone wall once more, and follow a short section of clear path for 100m until it turns to the left (an option to cut this long route in half).

East Canna only

To return to Canna Harbour, turn left and follow a path marked with plastic orange/red arrows (pointing in the opposite direction, as this is the route to the souterrain from the main track) south for 500m. When you reach the track running along the south coast, turn left and walk east for 3.5km, ignoring a turning to the left for the campsite, and turning left onto the track around **Canna Harbour** to return to Canna community shop.

West Canna only

To walk around the west of Canna from Canna Harbour, starting from Canna community shop, walk 1km south-west following the track around the harbour until just before the penultimate house before the bridge across to Sanday. Turn right through a gateway here, following a plastic orange/red arrow and sign for Canna Campsite, and walk west along a track for 2.5km (ignore the right turn to the campsite). As the track trends inland opposite Sgeir Chrioman, where a burn flows under the track through a plastic culvert towards a tiny sandy beach below, look out for a right turn onto an obvious path marked by a red/orange arrows. Follow this path north for 500m until an arrow points to your right, east (the path leads over a small hillock to the souterrain, 100m away). Instead, to continue to the west coast of Canna, turn left (west) and leave the marked path behind, continuing to follow the route described below.

Main route

To continue along the north coast, walk 50m west towards a small settlement of ruined sheiling huts visible in a grassy clearing. Continue 80m west over rough moor grass to a second collection of shielings in another grassy clearing where the parallel ridges of lazy beds are apparent. From the shielings, continue west and follow a faint trodden path over the saddle between two low hillocks. Descend south-west from the saddle, crossing a low drystone wall and a small burn in a deep ditch, making for the junction between a fence and a high drystone wall.

Rather than trapping yourself in the stone sheep pen here, step over a low part in the fence on your right and walk through a metal gate in the drystone wall a few metres further north, entering a low-lying open field on the north coast. Head south-west across the field to a gate at the junction between a wall and a stock fence. Go through the gate and turn right, trending west-north-west across boggy ground to regain height.

Find and follow a vague trodden path some distance landward of the northern cliffs, soon turning south along a stock fence above the Allt na Crìche Tuatha. Cross the fence by a step stile, then cross the burn and head to the clifftops before following them west. After 450m cross a burn and, on arriving at another burn after a further 750m (NG 216 056), descend from the clifftops to the raised shore platform via a distinct path initially on the east of the burn, before crossing it beside a drystone wall near the bottom.

Sgorr nam Bàn-naomha below the cliffs on the south-west coast

It is well worth abandoning the clifftops to explore this undercliff domain; the remains of shielings, walled enclosures and the corrugations of ancient lazy beds are testament to the struggle of **Canna's earlier inhabitants**, eking a living from the land. A dazzling outcrop of white shell sand makes for the perfect spot to sit and admire the fine views back along the cliffs to the east.

It is both possible and worthwhile to continue along the shore platform as far as **Garrisdale Point**; the dramatic coastal landscape is not far above sea level, and the views are impressive. A short way to the south, standing clear of the cliffs, is the once-fortified rock stack of Dùn Channa. The lighthouse on the islet of Hyskeir – or Òigh-sgeir – is visible 10km to the south-west and the strung-out archipelago of the Western Isles is visible on the horizon.

From Garrisdale Point, retrace your steps north-east for 250m and climb back to the clifftops by way of the obvious grassy slopes. You will have to step over a stock fence before the final crags give way to the clifftops. Continue along the clifftops, now enjoying a bird's eye view over Dùn Channa, climbing gently south to arrive at the high-cliff summit and trig point at **Sròn Ruail** (129m), with its commanding views over the Sea of the Hebrides and along Canna's southern cliffs.

Continue along an obvious, trodden path initially leading south-east along the clifftops – the going is generally easier along the southern cliffs with less heather, although the ground can be boggy at times. Descend a short way to cross a burn and continue along the clifftop as the view over to Rùm's north-western hills opens up magnificently.

Around 1.8km beyond Sròn Ruail, cross a burn, step over a fence on a wooden stile and climb to the dramatic clifftop summit of **Am Beannan**, which has spectacular views of Canna's eastern end and Sanday.

CLIFF OF THE HOLY WOMEN

To the east of Am Beannan on the raised shore platform beneath Sgorr nam Bàn-naomha (Cliff of the Holy Women) are the remains of a walled enclosure, thought to have been an early Christian monastic hermitage – possibly a nunnery, hence the name.

A fixed rope aids access to the shore platform, but descending is an 'assess-the-risk-yourself' situation, as rope or posts could deteriorate between the time of writing and your visit. Regardless, it should only be attempted in good conditions, with due caution, by one person at a time. If you still fancy the prospect, take care to watch the line of the rope above you as you descend, because it can dislodge loose rocks.

From Am Beannan, continue north-east along the cliffs, crossing three small burns in succession until you reach a gate in a drystone wall below Gualann Sgorr an Duine. Go through the gate and follow a grassy track which soon begins to descend gently, sweeping around to the north above the coastline as it cuts in to Canna's wasp waist at **Tarbert Bay**. Contour along above **Tota Tarra**, heading for a gateway in a stock fence, and the track to the north-east of a long stone building.

Join the track, which heads through a gate and climbs a short way before descending to the raised shore platform again and continuing its winding way for 4km back to **Canna Harbou**r. There is plenty to enjoy along the route with great views across Sanday to Rùm, miniature sandy beaches with clear turquoise water, and usually plenty of activity from seabirds, waders and divers. With luck or forethought, you'll arrive when the lovely Café Canna (licensed café and restaurant) is open to enjoy a reviving beverage.

WALK 22
Around Sanday

Start/finish	Bridge between Canna and Sanday (NG 266 050)
Time	3–4hr; shorter alternative via 'puffin path' 2hr 30min–3hr 30min
Distance	9.3km (5.8 miles); shorter alternative via 'puffin path' 7.8km (4.8 miles)
Total ascent	125m (410ft); shorter alternative via 'puffin path' 75m (245ft)
Difficulty	Quite easy going compared to the coast of Canna, there is a bit of rough ground to cover, but nothing too arduous
Terrain	Grassy coastal paths with some rough ground
Maps	OS Explorer 397; OS Landranger 39; Harvey Maps, Rùm, Eigg, Canna, Muck Superwalker XT25

After a demanding day-walk along Canna's towering cliffs, Sanday provides a perfect opportunity to take things a little easier with this half-day ramble around its gentle, low-lying coast. In fact, a walk around Sanday is the perfect diversion while awaiting an afternoon ferry to Mallaig or one of the other Small Isles.

Chief among this smaller island's attractions are the impressive rock stacks of Dùn Mòr and Dùn Beag, which are alive with nesting seabirds including puffins from the end of April to July – binoculars are handy to get a closer look. The views across the Sound of Canna to Bloodstone Hill, Orval and Fionchra on Rùm are worth the visit to Sanday alone.

Having crossed the **bridge** between Canna and Sanday, turn right, passing a Marian shrine with a stained-glass Madonna and child. Walk south-west on a path above a rocky shore and after a short distance you'll reach a small, beautiful sandy beach; cross this and make for a wooden gate above its south-western end. Go through the gate, turn right and walk inside the fence line until it ends, then follow a path just above the coastline trending west then south-west around **Sliabh na Creige Àirde**.

Walking Rùm and the Small Isles

This intricate coastline provides a range of different **habitats**, with bony lichen and barnacle-encrusted basalt formations creating tidal pools, and rocky islets offshore separated by deep channels of protected kelp forest.

As you approach Sanday's highest point at **Tallabric** (59m), follow a vague path climbing up to the clifftops. On a clear day, this elevated vantage point provides some fine views across Sanday and Canna's southern cliffs as well as onto Rùm, Coll, Tiree and the lighthouse on Hyskeir – or Òigh-sgeir.

Descend east along the clifftop keeping inside a stock fence. When you arrive above a rocky bay, walk north-east across a level field and follow a vague path to a metal gate in a fence running alongside a low stone wall.

Go through the gate, turn right and follow an intermittent grassy path around the low-lying coastline, then skirt around the seaward flank of Cnoc Ghreannabric, rising above low cliffs with excellent views across the bay at **Sùileabhaig** with the easternmost part of Sanday and Rùm beyond. Sùileabhaig is popular with grey seals; bobbing in the bay, they seem to follow your progress with curiosity as you walk around the shoreline.

As you approach the end of a small ridge, descend to your left (north), following a trodden path to a metal gate in a stock fence. Continue around the bay, skirting above the pebble beach, which is sadly one of the ocean's plastic dumping grounds. As the grassy plateau by the shore peters out, climb up to the low clifftop and follow it as it turns sharply north-east before descending to follow a drystone wall along to a gate. Go through the gate and follow a track straight ahead (east) for a short way before turning south to pass to the right of a lochan at An t-Oban, which has a small area of reed marsh decorated with yellow flag irises in late spring. The ground in this area is often churned up by cattle and is prone to bogginess, but there are some stepping stones across the outflow of the lochan.

Walk 22 – Around Sanday

Continue to follow the coast south-east, some distance back from the shore, passing the scant remains of an **Iron Age fort** on your right, before climbing up to the clifftops as they rise once again. Keep to the higher ground as the cliffs trend east-north-east, being somewhat wary of the edge which is severely undercut by erosion in parts – you'll soon be looking on to the rock stacks of Dùn Mòr and Dùn Beag. Continue along the clifftop, descending then climbing a little to arrive at a vantage point with the closest view of the rock stacks.

In season, puffins nest in deep burrows or crevices on the **rock stacks**, and can sometimes be seen in large numbers on the grassy plateau on top of Dùn Mòr, swooping around in flocks or floating in 'rafts' out to sea.

Alternative route

To cut the walk shorter by 1.5km and avoid some rough ground, the obvious 'puffin path' indicated with orange markers leads north-west for 1.5km to St Edwards Church. Follow it 200m inland until you are just south of the bay at Camas Stianabhaig. The route from Camas Stianabhaig back to the bridge is described below.

Main route

From the sea stacks viewpoint, descend directly north a short distance then cross a plank bridge over a muddy channel running into the head of an inlet, which

The Ceann an Eilein Beacon

frames a dramatic view of Dùn Beag. Continue around the headland inland from Garbh Sgeir on a narrow path along the coast. Turn north and pass to the landward side of the small, white Ceann an Eilein light beacon. Don't forget to look out for basking sharks and cetaceans off the coast (harbour porpoises are particularly frequent visitors).

Follow the coastline north to the narrow inlet inland of Uamh Ruadh then find a path heading west, contouring inland between rocky knolls towards Camas Stianabhaig – the ground can be boggy in places. Above Camas Stianabhaig, join the orange waymarked 'puffin trail' heading north-west (this is where the alternative shortcut, above, rejoins the main route). Follow this path for 600m, climbing over the brow of a low hill, towards the gate in a drystone wall above Sùileabhaig, passing the reedy lochan at An t-Oban on your left. Go through the gate and continue along the path north-west for 700m – **St Edwards Church** makes an obvious landmark to aim towards. Approaching the church, follow a drystone wall along to a gate on its east side and go through it.

> Standing alone on an elevated part of the island, the deconsecrated **Catholic church of St Edward** is the largest and most conspicuous building on Sanday. It was built in 1890, after the Clearances on Canna, when there was a much larger Catholic community on Sanday, and was also used by visiting fishermen from Barra and Eriskay. Unfortunately, the building has always had problems with damp and has long since fallen into disrepair.

Follow a path continuing north-west along the coast, passing a ruined house on your right (ignore the main track heading south-west unless the tide is very high, when you can follow it back to the bridge). Walk down towards the shore across from Eilean a' Bhàird where there is a gate in the fence.

> **Eilean a' Bhàird** (Island of the Bard) is named after Alasdair mac Mhaighstir Alasdair, who supposedly composed his greatest song while sheltering there under an upturned boat in the 18th century.

After going through the gate, turn left and follow a track skirting the shoreline, passing the small collection of houses until you arrive at the **bridge** once more.

MUCK

Looking north-west to Beinn Airein across the rugged inlet of Sloc na Dubhaich (Walk 23)

Port Mòr

MUCK

Muck is the smallest and most fertile of the Small Isles, measuring approximately 4km east to west and 2.5km north to south at its widest point. It lies 4km south-west of Eigg and is 13km north of Ardnamurchan, the westernmost point on the mainland of Britain. The lowest lying of the island group, its high point is Beinn Airein (137m).

When the weather is clement there can be few British islands as idyllic as Muck. Even when the ferry has delivered a batch of visitors outnumbering the island's population, Muck's tranquil air remains little disturbed. In high winds, however, the picture can be very different with little shelter to be found from the full fury of storms blowing in off the Atlantic. Nevertheless, Muck's low profile also allows for some tremendous views across to the mountainous aspects of Rùm and Eigg as well as the mainland coast.

Muck has been owned by the MacEwen family since 1896 and most of the island is run as a single livestock farm. The population of 30 mostly lives near the harbour at Port Mòr. The other settlement is the farm at Gallanach on Muck's north coast. The island's only road, which is about 2.5km long, connects the two. Muck is known for its seal population, and for the porpoises in its surrounding waters. In fact, the name may derive from the Gaelic word for porpoise, *muc mara* – literally, 'sea pig'.

MUCK

Owing to its small size, the island can be walked around in 6hr or less; the circumambulation, as described here, starts at Port Mòr and heads anticlockwise around the coast, taking in the headland of Am Maol, Gallanach Bay, Beinn Airein, Camas Mòr and Caisteal an Dùin Bhàin before returning to Port Mòr. The other, shorter, routes include some of Muck's highlights including Beinn Airein and Caisteal an Dùin Bhàin.

GEOLOGY

Muck is largely composed of basalt lava flows originating from Tertiary Period volcanic centres on Ardnamurchan and Rùm. These lava flows are clearly visible in step-like features comprising small escarpments formed from the hard, slow-cooling core of each flow, with gentler slopes between composed of the softer, more easily eroded rock formed above and below the core.

Beneath the basalts are a series of sandstones, limestones and shales formed during the Jurassic Period. On Muck, these are exposed on the shore at Camus Mòr, where you can see vast

Some of Camas Mòr's interesting geology can be seen from Beinn Airein (Walk 24)

Eigg beyond the tidal island of Coralag from Gallanach (Walks 23 and 24)

numbers of fossils. Doleritic basalt dikes are common on Muck; these were formed by upwelling magma filling fissures in the Earth's crust radiating out from centres of volcanic eruption. Erosion of the less-resistant rock they are intruded into has left them exposed as natural walls, giving rise to the broken coastline of Muck. There is also a large gabbro dike on the east side of Fang Mòr. The processes of glaciation removed much of the pre-glacial soils from the island. However, these have been replaced by loam soils produced by rapid weathering of the country rock combined with windblown sand.

HISTORY

Burial cairns at Àird nan Uan on the west side of Gallanach date from the Neolithic or early Bronze Age (about 2000BCE). On the peninsula south-west of Port Mòr, overlooking the harbour entrance, a Bronze Age fortification known as Caisteal an Dùin Bhàin ('Castle of the White Fort') sits atop a volcanic bluff – a cylindrical upthrust of rock with vertical cliffs 6m high all round. The structure incorporates a perimeter wall, two staggered gateways and internal walls.

Muck was probably settled by the Norsemen. There are many Norse place names throughout the Small Isles – including the hills of Rùm and the valleys of Eigg – but in Muck only the names Taolun and Sròn na Teiste are partially Norse in origin. Possible evidence of Norse settlement on Muck are the recently discovered vestiges of a large oval building at Toaluinn (or Taolun).

In the earliest account of Muck, from 1549, Sir Donald Munro, High Dean of the Isles, wrote that the island was 'very fertile and fruitful' with good fishing and 'one good Highland haven in it'. In the 1630s, the MacLeans of Coll took possession of Muck from the MacIans of Ardnamurchan. MacLean lairds continued to rule until the late 18th century when the incumbent laird ran into debt, which was paid off by Clanranald in exchange for the island.

In 1816 MacLean of Coll bought back Muck from Clanranald's trustees. At this time, kelp farming was an important source of income for the island, but the price of kelp declined and MacLean was soon in debt. The population of Muck had reached its peak of 320: in 1828 the MacLeans evicted 150 people who were transported on the *St Lawrence* from Tobermory to Cape Breton in Nova Scotia. By 1835 the remaining population had either emigrated or migrated elsewhere in Scotland.

In 1896 the island was bought by Lawrence Thomson, then owner of Eigg. The farmhouse was enlarged and the present farm cottages and barns were built. Thomson died in 1913 and the island passed to his brother, John MacEwen, who let the farm to tenants for a few years until his death in 1916; it was then inherited by Commander William MacEwen RN.

After the commander's death in 1967, Muck passed to his eldest son, Alasdair, who ran the island as a farm before moving to the mainland. The farm was subsequently taken over by his brother, Lawrence, who lived on Muck until his death in 2022. Lawrence's son Colin and his wife Ruth have been managing the farm since 2007.

WILDLIFE

Other than livestock and Highland ponies, there are no large land mammals on Muck. Otters live and breed in small numbers around the island. Rats feed on shellfish. Short-tailed voles are common, long-tailed field

A memorial dedicated to two islanders and a student who drowned near Horse Island while trying to shoot stags

Ringed plover chicks (Mary-Ann Featherstone)

mice and pygmy shrews less so. There are no reptiles on Muck and the only amphibian is the common toad.

Atlantic grey seals can be seen near Fionn-Àird and Port Mòr and along the north shore, principally at Godag, Port Chreadhain and Eilean nan Each, where small numbers of pups are born every autumn. Common seals occur in smaller numbers. Porpoises were once common, particularly in Gallanach Bay, and they can still be seen in the surrounding waters, while pods of dolphins sometimes pass, and killer whales (orca) are occasionally spotted. Minke whales are regularly sighted around the island between July and September. Basking sharks are seasonal visitors, feeding in the plankton-rich coastal waters.

Muck has a large number of seabirds, which nest predominantly on the islands of Eagamol and Eilean nan Each, as well as around the coastal cliffs and caves. There are Manx shearwaters, guillemots, razorbills, fulmars, gannets, cormorants, shags, terns and many varieties of gull, as well as small numbers of puffins. Passage migrants are also numerous, some of which overwinter, including turnstones and bar-tailed godwits, greylag, white-fronted and brent geese.

Insect life abounds on Muck, partly because insecticides are not used on the island. The relative lack of both shelter and calm days means that midges and clegs (horse flies) are comparatively scarce – a rare phenomenon in the Inner Hebrides. Butterflies and moths are abundant and occasional rare species such as the transparent burnet moth are to be found.

WOODLAND, PLANTS AND FLOWERS

Muck is low-lying and fertile with over 40 hectares (100 acres) of cultivated land. Most of the island is pasture, with expanses of bracken in some areas and heather cover in Gleann Mhairtein. There is no native woodland on Muck, but hazel and birch remains found in a small peat bog near Gallanach show that it was present in the distant past. Aside from a few poplars on the cliffs west of Port Mòr, Muck was treeless until 1922, when three small plantations were established to provide shelter and fuel. Subsequent plantations have incorporated the more common British species and, provided with shelter, these have thrived. The success of the Sitka spruce is evident in several towering specimens.

From late spring through summer the island has abundant plant life. Meadowsweet, flag iris, golden silverweed, thistle, bell heather, saxifrage, tormentil and various umbellifers are among the common plants encountered in the island's different habitats. Surprisingly, a few alpine plants are found, 600m below their usual altitude: dwarf juniper, crowberry, club moss, rose root sedum, mountain cats-paw and pyramidal bugle. Among the less common plants found on Muck are thyme broomrape, the frog orchid and small white orchid.

GETTING AROUND

Visitors are not permitted to bring vehicles to Muck without special permission; there is no public transport on the island and only 3km of road anyway. Getting around on foot or by bicycle are the main options.

AMENITIES

The Isle of Muck's website (www.isleofmuck.com) provides useful information about amenities, accommodation and other aspects of the island.

There is no grocery shop, so you should bring your own supplies – there is a small Co-op supermarket in Mallaig. With the exception of Gallanach Lodge, all Muck's amenities are in the main village, Port Mòr. The Tea Room (tel 07470 711799 chocnesschocolates@gmail.com) is open seasonally for lunch and some evenings; call or email ahead to confirm opening times. It serves home-made food using locally sourced produce including shellfish, home baking, sandwiches and soup. The Community Hall (tel 01687 462362 info@isleofmuck.com) – a black building next to the school – has facilities including Wi-Fi, toilets and showers (honesty-box payments), a small heritage centre and a games room. The Green Shed craft shop (24hr with honesty box) also

The Green Shed gift shop in Port Mòr (Walks 23 and 25)

sells a range of locally produced arts and crafts.

Gallanach Lodge (see below), in the north of the island, welcomes non-residents for evening meals if not fully booked, but you must call ahead.

PLACES TO STAY

Conveniently located in Port Mòr, the Bunkhouse (tel 01687 462362 www.isleofmuck.com) is a small, modern, purpose-built wooden building with three bunk rooms and one double room. There's a light, comfortable communal area, fully equipped kitchen, shower, toilets and washing machine. It fills up quite quickly in summer.

On the north coast, Gallanach Lodge (tel 01687 462365 www.gallanachlodge.co.uk) is a more upmarket option with eight rooms, a grand, open-plan sitting room and dining area. Rates include breakfast and a three-course dinner.

For self-catering, there are three well-appointed and scenically situated holiday cottages (tel 01687 462362 www.isleofmuck.com) available to let year-round, variously sleeping up to five, six or seven people.

WALK 23
Around Muck

Start/finish	The old pier opposite Pier House in Port Mòr (NM 422 793)
Time	4hr 30min–6hr; western Muck only 3hr 45min–5hr; eastern Muck only 1–2hr
Distance	14.8km (9.2 miles); western Muck only 12.3km (7.6 miles); eastern Muck only 5km (3.1 miles)
Total ascent	300m (985ft); western Muck only 275m (900ft); eastern Muck only 60m (195ft)
Difficulty	More difficult than it might seem, this route covers some rough ground as well as requiring navigational care at times
Terrain	Soft, springy turf, moor grass and low heather with indistinct trodden paths, boggy patches and a number of stock fences to be crossed
Maps	OS Explorer 397; OS Landranger 39; Harvey Maps, Rùm, Eigg, Canna, Muck Superwalker XT25

An anticlockwise circumambulation of Muck's entire coastline, this walk takes in changing landscapes with diverse terrain and constantly shifting views of the neighbouring islands and mainland mountains. After the low-lying east coast, the cliffs and rough, rocky moorland in the far west and south are a remarkable contrast – these wild and often dramatic landscapes can feel surprisingly remote.

Walking around the entire island in one go is perfectly manageable for fit walkers, but shouldn't be underestimated. The route can be shortened by 2.5km and as much as 1hr's walk by omitting the easternmost part of the coastline and walking across the island from Port Mòr to Gallanach along the single-track road, which sees very little traffic. Walking the east coast separately and returning via the road makes for a quick leg stretcher if time allows on ferry day.

From the **old pier** opposite Pier House, walk north along the road for 30m, then turn right joining a track that climbs gently south-east away from the road, passing to the right of a house. Go through a stock gate, pass a shed and two houses

before turning left off the main track past allotment gardens. Continue along the track as it bends south-east again and passes along the outside of a fence.

When the track reaches a gate, do not go through it, but instead keep to the shore side of a fence initially lined with small trees. Keeping the fence on your left, trend around a small headland following a lightly trodden path, which is indicated in a couple of places with black arrows. Go through a small metal gate and stay on higher ground walking above low clifftops on the outside of fenced fields, until you reach a gully where you have to step over two sections of fence to reach the gully's edge (the first section doesn't have a stile while, 10m further on, the second one does).

Skirt around the gully and continue walking around the coast following an indistinct path which contours along above low cliffs in view of the sea. Stay above an area of rough, boggy ground, before walking along the edge of some ancient lazy beds to rejoin the low clifftops as the coastline turns north-west at Eilean Dubh. Look out for the entrance to a cave in the cliff – visible from above – just north of Eilean Dubh.

Walk north-north-west following the clifftops with great views of Eigg, Moidart and Morar only slightly marred by the distinctive circular pens of a fish

WALK 23 – AROUND MUCK

farm. Just opposite the fish farm, pass through a metal gate on the clifftop and continue to the small headland of **Am Maol**. This fine vantage point looks across the Sound of Eigg to the striking pitchstone ridge of An Sgùrr, with Rùm to the north.

From the neck of Am Maol, continue past the rocky beach at Port nam Maol, following a path to gain higher ground on the sea side of a boggy lochan, then continue along a grassy area by the coast, passing some 200m below a white house.

Continue along the coast a little way back from the shore, following a trodden path where useful. Above Port na Lice, cross a burn flowing through a man-made channel and make for a drystone wall and fence where it abuts a basalt dike near the shore. Climb over the wall at the point where it meets the natural rock (or walk round the dike on the shore if the tide is low enough), turn left and go through a stock gate into a field. Walk diagonally (south-west) across the field on a slight rise to go through another stock gate. Turn right (north-west), then continue around to the point of the low clifftop at Toaluinn for a view north-west to Eilean nan Each beyond the tip of the narrow Àird nan Uan peninsula – Rùm looms large on the horizon.

From the point, head back inland and descend towards a gate in a drystone wall above the beach at **Camas na Cairidh**. Go through the gate, turn left and climb a short way to join the road.

Camas na Cairidh on the north coast

The MacEwen family grave on the Àird nan Uan peninsula, sited on a prehistoric cairn

East Muck only
To return to **Port Mòr** from here, turn left and walk south-south-east along the road for 1.2km.

West Muck only
Alternatively, to omit the east of Muck from this walk, start by walking 1.2km north-north-west along the road from **Port Mòr** and continue the route instructions from here.

Main route
Walk westwards along the road and arrive at **Gallanach Bay** after 600m. Explore the beach, then continue around the bay past **Gallanach farm**, a second, smaller beach, and further farm buildings. Where the road ends, follow a path north-north-west as it rises towards a cottage perched idyllically above the shore.

Cross a stile on the left just before you reach the house, climb a short way and pass through the gap at the corner of a drystone wall and fence, turn right (north-north-west) and walk out along the **Àird nan Uan peninsula** following a path to the narrow, tide-separated isthmus connecting Eilean nan Uan ('Lamb Island'). There is a good view on to Eilean nan Each ('Horse Island').

WALK 23 – AROUND MUCK

There are several **cairns** on the Àird nan Uan peninsula, most likely from the Bronze Age; the one furthest north has also been used as the MacEwen family grave.

Return south-south-east along the peninsula, keeping to higher ground to avoid awkward terrain, before following a boggy path to cross above the head of the inlet on its western side. Make for a rustic-looking grass-roofed bothy standing back from the shore.

From the bothy, follow a path north-west along the coast for 250m to arrive at a beach composed entirely of small shells. Climb south just above the beach and over a short section of drystone wall. Continue south-west along the coast, soon joining a distinct track that contours above the shore, beneath the low craggy cliffs at Achadh na Creige. Follow the track south across a low-lying area before it crosses the neck of a promontory (NM 398 797) – here, leave the track bearing right and head towards the shore north of **Gleann Mhairtein**.

Continue over low ground and cross a burn before ascending again above low cliffs in Muck's westernmost corner. Gain height as the coastline turns south above **Rubh' Leam na Làraich**, climbing steadily on a distinct path along the increasingly dramatic clifftops. There are fine views down to the rugged coastline below and across to Ardnamurchan, Mull, Coll and Tiree.

Follow the clifftop path south-east and descend a little before climbing again to the high clifftop above **Sròn na Teiste**. Turn left (north-north-east) and head towards the looming bulk of **Beinn Airein**. Descend a short way before climbing steeply, following an obvious path which leads up diagonally through a craggy cliff to a grassy plateau. Here, bear right towards a row of fence posts running along the western clifftops; approaching these, turn left and climb steeply along the line of the cliff to gain the summit (137m) marked with an OS **trig pillar**. Beinn Airein is a fine vantage point with 360-degree views over Muck and across to the surrounding islands and mainland.

Descend north-north-east on a grassy slope avoiding rocky areas around the summit. Continue descending along the clifftop inside the stock fence until your progress is interrupted by a fence. Follow this fence 100m inland to a gate – go through and continue to descend finding the most sensible line down grassy slopes to the rocky beach at **Camas Mòr**.

After taking some time to explore the beach and its fossils (Walk 24), walk north (inland) for 150m then bear right (east), to go through a gate in a drystone wall just to the right of a stone sheepfold – crossing over the neck of the jutting promontory at Torr nam Fitheach. From the gate, walk south-east towards the shore until you reach a fence which can be crossed over a stile. Turn left and walk on the shore side of the fence until it reaches a gravel track. Turn right onto the

The north-west coast

track and follow it for 80m before leaving it to the right and heading towards the clifftops. Guillemots, razorbills and shags nest on the cliffs around the caves here.

Walk south-east, following the line of the cliffs until you reach the headland on the north side of **Sloc na Dubhaich**. Walk across the neck of this headland and follow a path some distance inland as it contours around Muck's most southerly point.

Descend to shore level by a bothy as the coastline morphs from clifftops to parallel skerries, then head around the undulating shoreline to Caisteal an Dùin Bhàin (Walk 25). From here, head north up over the rough, rocky moorland of Dùn Bàn until you reach a track; turn right onto the track and continue around the bay to **Port Mòr**.

WALK 24
Beinn Airein and Camas Mòr

Start/finish	Gallanach (NM 409 802)
Time	1hr 30min–2hr 30min
Distance	5km (3.1 miles)
Total ascent	150m (490ft)
Difficulty	A short walk covering some rough ground and requiring careful navigation at times
Terrain	Moorland with indistinct trodden paths and boggy patches, followed by a rocky shore and then farmland on the return
Maps	OS Explorer 397; OS Landranger 39; Harvey Maps, Rùm, Eigg, Canna, Muck Superwalker XT25

This rewarding circuit summits Muck's highest hill, explores some interesting coastline and cuts southwards across the island through a moorland valley. The three beaches visited during the walk each have their own distinctive charms. To begin and end the walk, the fine sands of Gallanach Bay stretch out to the tidal island of Coralag; further west a secluded shell beach is hidden among the skerries; and, after descending Beinn Airein, the dramatic, rocky Camas Mòr has a fascinating array of fossils under its towering cliffs. Despite a modest height of 137m, Beinn Airein itself has spectacular views of the surrounding islands and mountainous West Highland peninsulas.

From **Gallanach Bay**, continue west along the road past two sets of farm buildings, Just beyond the second, go through small gate in a stone wall on your left and walk over a rise. Join a track for a short distance before heading west across the neck of the **Àird nan Uan peninsula** towards a grass-roofed bothy, staying on higher ground away from the shore to avoid the worst of the bogginess.

From the bothy, follow a path north-west along the coast for 250m to arrive at a small beach made of shells. Fertile Eilean nan Each ('Horse Island') lies just off the coast, with the Rùm Cuillin on the skyline beyond. Camouflaged ringed plovers nest here, so be careful where you tread and keep dogs on leads in spring.

From here, climb just above the beach and continue over a short section of drystone wall. Head inland along an indistinct trodden path, climbing for 200m, then turn right to follow a track, as it contours above the shore beneath the low

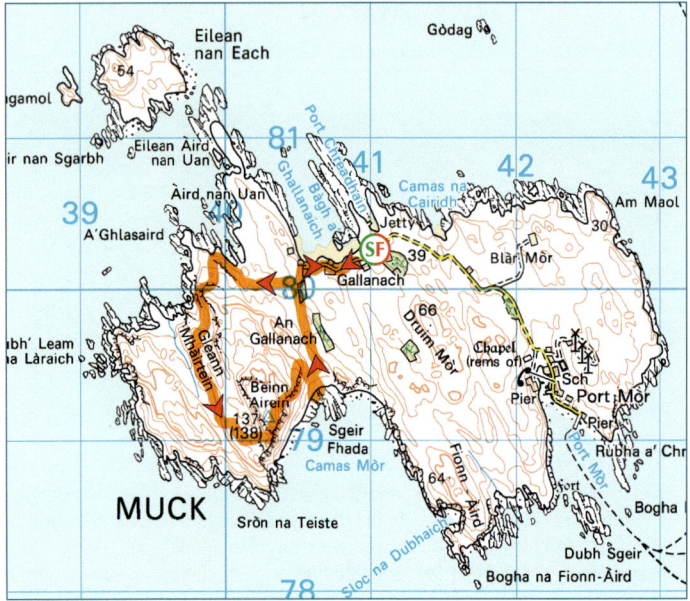

cliffs of Achadh na Creige then heads south (inland) over an area of low ground. Walk over a rise at the neck of a rocky promontory and continue heading south up the east side of the broad **Gleann Mhàirtein** valley following a dirt then trodden grass path along higher ground as it gently rises.

Where the valley begins to narrow as it approaches the south-west coast of Muck, take a path bearing left that climbs steeply through rocks up onto a grassy plateau on the south-west side of **Beinn Airein**. From here, turn right and walk towards a line of fence posts along the cliffs on the hill's southern flank – a distinct path then leads up the steepest part of the ascent to the summit OS **trig point** (137m).

Beinn Airein has panoramic views across the whole of Muck, the other Small Isles, Ardnamurchan, Coll, Tiree and Mull, while also providing an aerial perspective over Camas Mòr's striking geology, where sedimentary Jurassic limestones are overlain by lava flows from the Palaeogene period.

A picnic on Camas Mòr

Descend north-east on a grassy slope avoiding the crags around the summit. Follow the line of the clifftop as it loses height, keeping inside the stock fence until your descent is interrupted by another fence. Follow this fence 100m north (inland) to a gate. Go through the gate and continue to descend finding the most sensible route down grassy slopes to the rocky beach at **Camas Mòr**.

Camas Mòr is a designated Site of Special Scientific Interest (SSSI) due to its innumerable and varied fossils. These date from between 60 million and 3 billion years ago, with the most obvious and abundant being gryphaea, a type of oyster also known as 'devil's toenails'.

From the beach, head north from directly between Beinn Airein and Torr nam Fitheach to a gate in a stock fence; walk through it into a field.

Cross this field north-north-west towards a small copse of trees in its far north corner, then cross a stile over a fence on the left-hand side of the trees. Cross a plank over a burn and continue north with the trees on your right over an area of lumpy, higher ground until you reach the original track from the start of the walk. Turn right onto the track, which leads to the left of the farm buildings – to avoid the farm itself, leave the track just before the buildings and head to the left side of a fence over a small rise, where you will soon find the small gate where the walk began. From here, turn right onto the road to return to **Gallanach Bay**.

Gallanach Bay with the tidal island Coralag and a distant Rùm

WALK 25
Caisteal an Dùin Bhàin and the far south coast

Start/finish	The old pier opposite Pier House in Port Mòr (NM 422 793)
Time	1–2hr
Distance	4.5km (2.8 miles)
Total ascent	80m (260ft)
Difficulty	A fairly easy ramble without good paths
Terrain	Coastal moorland with some boggy patches and rocky shore
Maps	OS Explorer 397; OS Landranger 39; Harvey Maps, Rùm, Eigg, Canna, Muck Superwalker XT25

With an abandoned village, ancient fort and ruined farmstead, this short walk takes in some of Muck's most interesting archaeological sites. There's also a great view across to Ardnamurchan and a sheltered tidal pool if you fancy a quick dip. Keep an eye out for seals, harbour porpoises and other cetaceans around the coast.

From the old pier opposite Pier House in **Port Mòr**, follow the road north for 250m until it turns to the left (west) at the head of **Port Mòr bay**. Stay on the road for a further 80m and, where the road turns north again at a junction, turn left onto a track leading south and stay with it for a few metres before leaving it to the right. Climb a small rise to explore the ruined settlement of **Sean Bhaile** which extends for 200m to the north-west.

Return to the track heading south on the west side of Port Mòr bay and continue a short distance until you reach a fork. Bear right here and continue 150m, following the track as it veers sharply right at a stone house with swings outside. After the next turning, leave the track and head south.

Walk up over Dùn Bàn – a raised area of rough, rocky moorland with a great view over Port Mòr – heading south-south-east for 700m to Caisteal an Dùin Bhàin. An obvious rounded lump, the top of this prehistoric fort is covered by grass, but there are some visible remains of manmade stone walls above the natural rock. Climbing on top is not difficult from the west side and proves to be an excellent viewpoint across the sound to Ardnamurchan. An Iron Age fort built on

WALKING RÙM AND THE SMALL ISLES

a basalt stack near the end of a rocky promontory, Caisteal an Dùin Bhàin guards the approach to the natural harbour at Port Mòr.

From here, continue west around the rocky shoreline for 450m, to the ruined farmstead of Leabaidh Dhonnchaidh (NM 419 787). Walk south-west around a narrow inlet to a metal-roofed bothy and continue 160m south following a narrow, raised shore platform to a series of deep, tidal pools, one of which is known as the Mermaid's Pool and has been a popular swimming spot for generations of islanders. At low tide, you can walk a little further around the coast to a miniature sandy beach beneath the cliffs.

To return to Port Mòr, retrace your steps to the metal-roofed bothy, walk to the Leabaidh Dhonnchaidh ruins and then head north-north-east across low-lying fields before climbing back over Dùn Bàn to the track. Turn right and follow the track, then road around the bay back to **Port Mòr**.

Ruins of Sean Bhaile in front of Port Mòr

SEAN BHAILE

Consisting of at least 48 buildings from different periods with adjoining enclosures and a stone-walled street, Sean Bhaile (also known as Kiel or A'Chill) has a complex history and is the best example of an old settlement on the island.

The rubble remains of a chapel and burial ground to the south-east of the ruined settlement suggest the site has been in use since early Christian times, with two carved memorial stones attributed to the seventh and ninth centuries (one of these has been moved to the community hall).

More recent ruins date from the 19th century. In 1828 the landowning Clan MacLean cleared Muck and evicted 150 people who sailed on the *St Lawrence* from Tobermory to Cape Breton in Canada. The remaining inhabitants were allowed to build new houses in Sean Bhaile; they tried to sustain themselves through fishing, but by 1835 they had all left the island.

APPENDIX A
Useful websites

Islands

Canna
www.theisleofcanna.com

Eigg
http://isleofeigg.org

Muck
http://isleofmuck.com

Rùm
www.isleofrum.com

Visit Small Isles
www.visitsmallisles.com

General information

Hebridean Whale and Dolphin Trust
https://hwdt.org

Historic Environment Scotland – Canmore
https://canmore.org.uk

Isle of Rum Red Deer Project
https://rumdeer.bio.ed.ac.uk

National Trust for Scotland
www.nts.org.uk

NatureScot
www.nature.scot

Scottish Geology Trust
www.scottishgeologytrust.org

APPENDIX B
Further reading

Irvine Butterfield, *Dibidil: A Hebridean Adventure*, MBA, 2010

Archie Cameron, *Bare Feet and Tackety Boots*, Luath, 1988

John L. Campbell, *Canna: The Story of a Hebridean Island*, Birlinn, 2002

Gareth Cole, *Café Canna, Recipes from a Hebridean Island,* Birlinn, 2024

Camille Dressler, *Eigg: The Story of an Island*, Birlinn, 2007

John Hunter, *The Small Isles*, Historic Environment Scotland, 2016

John Love, *Rùm: A Landscape Without Figures*, Birlinn, 2002

Magnus Magnusson, *Rùm: Nature's Island*, Luath, 1997

Alan McKirdy, *The Small Isles, a Landscape in Stone*, Birlinn, 2022

DOWNLOAD THE GPX FILES

All the routes in this guide are available for download from:

www.cicerone.co.uk/1217/GPX

as standard format GPX files. You should be able to load them into most online GPX systems and mobile devices, whether GPS or smartphone. You may need to convert the file into your preferred format using a conversion programme such as gpsvisualizer.com or one of the many other such websites and programmes.

When you follow this link, you will be asked for your email address and where you purchased the guidebook, and have the option to subscribe to the Cicerone e-newsletter.

www.cicerone.co.uk

LISTING OF CICERONE GUIDES

BRITISH ISLES CHALLENGES, COLLECTIONS AND ACTIVITIES

Great Walks on the England Coast Path
Map and Compass
The Big Rounds
The Book of the Bivvy
The Book of the Bothy
The Mountains of England and Wales:
  Vol 1 Wales
  Vol 2 England
The National Trails
Walking the End to End Trail
Cycling Land's End to John o' Groats

SHORT WALKS SERIES

15 Short Walks Hadrian's Wall
15 Short Walks in the Lake District: Keswick, Borrowdale and Buttermere
15 Short Walks in the Lake District: Windermere Ambleside and Grasmere
15 Short Walks Lake District: Coniston and Langdale
15 Short Walks in Arnside and Silverdale
15 Short Walks in the Ribble Valley
15 Short Walks in Nidderdale
15 Short Walks in Northumberland: Wooler, Rothbury, Alnwick and the coast
15 Short Walks in the Yorkshire Dales: Grassington, Skipton, Malham and Ilkley
15 Short Walks in the Peak District: Bakewell and the White Peak
15 Short Walks on the Malvern Hills
15 Short Walks in Cornwall: Falmouth and the Lizard
15 Short Walks in Cornwall: Land's End and Penzance
15 Short Walks in the South Downs: Brighton, Eastbourne and Arundel
15 Short Walks in the Surrey Hills
15 Short Walks on Dartmoor North: Okehampton and Chagford
15 Short Walks on Dartmoor South: Ivybridge and Princetown
15 Short Walks on Exmoor
15 Short Walks Winchester
15 Short Walks in Bannau Brycheiniog: Brecon Beacons
15 Short Walks in Pembrokeshire: Tenby and the south
15 Short Walks in Dumfries and Galloway
15 Short Walks in the Trossachs: Callander and Aberfoyle
15 Short Walks on the Isle of Mull
15 Short Walks on the Orkney Islands
15 Short Walks on the Shetland Islands

SCOTLAND

Ben Nevis and Glen Coe
Cycling in the Hebrides
Cycling the North Coast 500
Great Mountain Days in Scotland
Mountain Biking in Southern and Central Scotland
Mountain Biking in West and North West Scotland
Not the West Highland Way: A Mountain High Way
Scotland
Scotland's Best Small Mountains
Scotland's Mountain Ridges
Scottish Wild Country Backpacking
Skye's Cuillin Ridge Traverse
The Borders Abbeys Way
The Great Glen Way
The Great Glen Way Map Booklet
The Hebridean Way
The Hebrides
The Isle of Mull
The Isle of Skye
The Skye Trail
The Southern Upland Way
The West Highland Way
The West Highland Way Map Booklet
Walking Ben Lawers, Rannoch and Atholl
Walking in the Cairngorms
Walking in the Pentland Hills
Walking in the Scottish Borders
Walking in the Southern Uplands
Walking in Torridon, Fisherfield, Fannichs and An Teallach
Walking Loch Lomond and the Trossachs
Walking on Arran
Walking on Harris and Lewis
Walking on Jura, Islay and Colonsay
Walking on Mull, Coll and Tiree
Walking on Rum and the Small Isles
Walking on the Orkney and Shetland Isles
Walking on Uist and Barra
Walking the Cape Wrath Trail
Walking the Corbetts
  Vol 1 South of the Great Glen
  Vol 2 North of the Great Glen
Walking the Fife Pilgrim Way
Walking the Galloway Hills
Walking the John o' Groats Trail
Walking the Munros
  Vol 1 Southern, Central and Western Highlands
  Vol 2 Northern Highlands and the Cairngorms
Winter Climbs in the Cairngorms
Winter Climbs: Ben Nevis and Glen Coe

NORTHERN ENGLAND ROUTES

Cycling the Reivers Route
Cycling the Way of the Roses
Hadrian's Cycleway
Hadrian's Wall Path
Hadrian's Wall Path Map Booklet
The Coast to Coast Cycle Route
The Coast to Coast Map Booklet
The Coast to Coast Walk
Walking the Dales Way
The Dales Way Map Booklet
Walking the Pennine Way
Pennine Way Map Booklet

LAKE DISTRICT

Bikepacking in the Lake District
Cycling in the Lake District
Great Mountain Days in the Lake District
Joss Naylor's Lakes, Meres and Waters of the Lake District
Lake District Winter Climbs
Lake District:
  High Level and Fell Walks
  Low Level and Lake Walks
Mountain Biking in the Lake District
Outdoor Adventures with Children — Lake District
Scrambles in the Lake District —
  North
  South
Trail and Fell Running in the Lake District
Walking The Cumbria Way
Walking the Lake District Fells —
  Borrowdale
  Buttermere
  Coniston
  Keswick
  Langdale
  Mardale and the Far East
  Patterdale
  Wasdale
Walking the Tour of the Lake District

NORTH-WEST ENGLAND AND THE ISLE OF MAN

Cycling the Pennine Bridleway
Isle of Man Coastal Path
The Lancashire Cycleway
The Lune Valley and Howgills
Walking in Cumbria's Eden Valley
Walking in Lancashire
Walking in the Forest of Bowland and Pendle
Walking on the Isle of Man
Walking on the West Pennine Moors
Walking the Ribble Way
Walks in Silverdale and Arnside

NORTH-EAST ENGLAND, YORKSHIRE DALES AND PENNINES

Cycling in the Yorkshire Dales
Great Mountain Days in the Pennines
Mountain Biking in the Yorkshire Dales
The Cleveland Way and the Yorkshire Wolds Way
The Cleveland Way Map Booklet
The North York Moors
Trail and Fell Running in the Yorkshire Dales
Walking in County Durham
Walking in Northumberland
Walking in the North Pennines
Walking in the Yorkshire Dales: North and East
  South and West
Walking St Cuthbert's Way
Walking St Oswald's Way and Northumberland Coast Path

DERBYSHIRE, PEAK DISTRICT AND MIDLANDS

Cycling in the Peak District
Dark Peak Walks
Scrambles in the Dark Peak
Walking in Derbyshire
Walking in the Peak District -
  White Peak East
  White Peak West

WALES AND WELSH BORDERS

Cycle Touring in Wales
Cycling Lon Las Cymru
Great Mountain Days in Snowdonia
Hillwalking in Shropshire
Mountain Walking in Snowdonia
Offa's Dyke Path
Offa's Dyke Map Booklet
Scrambles in Snowdonia
Snowdonia: 30 Low-level and Easy Walks — North, South
The Cambrian Way
The Pembrokeshire Coast Path
The Pembrokeshire Coast Path Map Booklet
The Snowdonia Way
The Wye Valley Walk
Walking Glyndwr's Way
Walking in Carmarthenshire
Walking in Pembrokeshire
Walking in the Brecon Beacons
Walking in the Wye Valley
Walking on Gower
Walking the Severn Way
Walking the Shropshire Way
Walking the Wales Coast Path

SOUTHERN ENGLAND

20 Classic Sportive Rides
  in South East England
  in South West England
Cycling in the Cotswolds
Mountain Biking on the North Downs
Mountain Biking on the South Downs
The North Downs Way
The North Downs Way Map Booklet
The South Downs Way
The South Downs Way Map Booklet
The Cotswold Way
The Cotswold Way Map Booklet
The Ridgeway National Trail
The Ridgeway Map Booklet
The Thames Path
The Thames Path Map Booklet
The Two Moors Way
Two Moors Way Map Booklet
Walking the South West Coast Path
South West Coast Path Map Booklet
  Vol 1: Minehead to St Ives
  Vol 2: St Ives to Plymouth
  Vol 2: St Ives to Plymouth
  Vol 3: Plymouth to Poole
Suffolk Coast and Heath Walks
The Kennet and Avon Canal
The Lea Valley Walk
The Peddars Way and Norfolk Coast Path
The Pilgrims' Way
Walking Hampshire's Test Way
Walking in Essex
Walking in Kent
Walking in London
Walking in Norfolk
Walking in the Chilterns
Walking in the Cotswolds
Walking in the Isles of Scilly
Walking in the New Forest
Walking in the North Wessex Downs
Walking on Dartmoor
Walking on Guernsey
Walking on Jersey
Walking on the Isle of Wight
Walking the Dartmoor Way
Walking the Jurassic Coast
Walking the Sarsen Way
Walks in the South Downs National Park

ALPS CROSS-BORDER ROUTES

100 Hut Walks in the Alps
Alpine Ski Mountaineering Vol 1 — Western Alps
The Karnischer Hohenweg
The Tour of the Bernina
Trail Running — Chamonix and the Mont Blanc region
Trekking Chamonix to Zermatt
Trekking in the Alps
Trekking in the Silvretta and Ratikon Alps
Trekking Munich to Venice
Trekking the Tour du Mont Blanc
Tour du Mont Blanc Map Booklet
Walking in the Alps

FRANCE, BELGIUM, AND LUXEMBOURG

Camino de Santiago — Via Podiensis
Chamonix Mountain Adventures
Cycling London to Paris
Cycling the Canal de la Garonne
Cycling the Canal du Midi

Mont Blanc Walks
Mountain Adventures in the Maurienne
Short Treks on Corsica
The GR5 Trail
The GR5 Trail —
  Vosges and Jura
  Benelux and Lorraine
The Moselle Cycle Route
Trekking in the Vanoise
Trekking the Cathar Way
Trekking the GR10
Trekking the GR20 Corsica
Trekking the Robert Louis Stevenson Trail
Via Ferratas of the French Alps
Walking in Provence — East
Walking in Provence — West
Walking in the Auvergne
Walking in the Briançonnais
Walking in the Dordogne
Walking in the Haute Savoie: North
Walking in the Haute Savoie: South
Walking on Corsica
Walking the Brittany Coast Path
Walking in the Ardennes

PYRENEES AND FRANCE/SPAIN CROSS-BORDER ROUTES

Shorter Treks in the Pyrenees
The Pyrenean Haute Route
The Pyrenees
Trekking the Cami dels Bons Homes
Trekking the GR11 Trail
Walks and Climbs in the Pyrenees

SPAIN AND PORTUGAL

Camino de Santiago: Camino Frances
Coastal Walks in Andalucia
Costa Blanca Mountain Adventures
Cycling the Camino de Santiago
Mountain Walking in Mallorca
Mountain Walking in Southern Catalunya
Spain's Sendero Historico: The GR1
The Andalucian Coast to Coast Walk
The Camino del Norte and Camino Primitivo
The Camino Ingles and Ruta do Mar
The Mountains Around Nerja
The Mountains of Ronda and Grazalema
The Sierras of Extremadura
Trekking in Mallorca
Trekking in the Canary Islands
Trekking the GR7 in Andalucia
Walking and Trekking in the Sierra Nevada
Walking in Andalucia
Walking in Catalunya —
  Barcelona
  Girona Pyrenees
Walking in the Picos de Europa
Walking La Via de la Plata and Camino Sanabres
Walking on Gran Canaria
Walking on La Gomera and El Hierro

Walking on La Palma
Walking on Lanzarote and Fuerteventura
Walking on Tenerife
Walking on the Costa Blanca
Walking the Camino dos Faros
Portugal's Rota Vicentina
The Camino Portugues
Walking in Portugal
Walking in the Algarve
Walking on Madeira
Walking on the Azores

SWITZERLAND
Switzerland's Jura Crest Trail
The Swiss Alps
Tour of the Jungfrau Region
Trekking the Swiss Via Alpina
Walking in Arolla and Zinal
Walking in the Bernese Oberland — Jungfrau region
Walking in the Engadine — Switzerland
Walking in Ticino
Walking in Zermatt and Saas-Fee

GERMANY
Hiking and Cycling in the Black Forest
The Danube Cycleway Vol 1
The Rhine Cycle Route
The Westweg
Walking in the Bavarian Alps

POLAND, SLOVAKIA, ROMANIA, HUNGARY AND BULGARIA
The Danube Cycleway Vol 2
The High Tatras
The Mountains of Romania

SCANDINAVIA, ICELAND AND GREENLAND
Hiking in Norway —
  North
  South
Trekking the Kungsleden
Trekking in Greenland — The Arctic Circle Trail
Walking and Trekking in Iceland

SLOVENIA, CROATIA, SERBIA, MONTENEGRO AND ALBANIA
Hiking Slovenia's Juliana Trail
Mountain Biking in Slovenia
The Islands of Croatia
The Julian Alps of Slovenia
The Mountains of Montenegro
The Peaks of the Balkans Trail
The Peaks of the Balkans Trail
The Slovene Mountain Trail
Walking in Slovenia: The Karavanke
Walks and Treks in Croatia

ITALY
Alta Via
  1 — Trekking in the Dolomites
  2 — Trekking in the Dolomites

Day Walks in the Dolomites
Italy's Grande Traversata delle Alpi
Italy's Sibillini National Park
Ski Touring and Snowshoeing in the Dolomites
The Way of St Francis: Via di Francesco
Trekking Gran Paradiso: Alta Via 2
Trekking in the Apennines
Trekking the Giants' Trail: Alta Via 1 through the Italian Pennine Alps
Via Ferratas of the Italian Dolomites:
  Vol 1
  Vol 2
Walking in Abruzzo
Walking in Italy's Cinque Terre
Walking in Italy's Stelvio National Park
Walking in Sicily
Walking in the Aosta Valley
Walking in the Dolomites
Walking in Tuscany
Walking in Umbria
Walking Lake Como and Maggiore
Walking Lake Garda and Iseo
Walking on the Amalfi Coast
Walking the Via Francigena Pilgrim Route
  Part 1
  Part 2
  Part 3
  Part 4
Walks and Treks in the Maritime Alps

IRELAND
The Wild Atlantic Way and Western Ireland
Walking the Kerry Way
Walking the Wicklow Way

EUROPEAN CYCLING
Cycling the Route des Grandes Alpes
Cycling the Ruta Via de la Plata
The Elbe Cycle Route
The River Loire Cycle Route
The River Rhone Cycle Route

INTERNATIONAL CHALLENGES, COLLECTIONS AND ACTIVITIES
Europe's High Points
Pocket First Aid and Wilderness Medicine

AUSTRIA
Innsbruck Mountain Adventures
Trekking Austria's Adlerweg
Trekking in Austria's Hohe Tauern
Trekking in Austria's Stubai Alps
Trekking in Austria's Zillertal Alps
Walking in Austria
Walking in the Salzkammergut: the Austrian Lake District

MEDITERRANEAN
The High Mountains of Crete
Trekking in Greece
Walking and Trekking in Zagori
Walking and Trekking on Corfu

Walking on the Greek Islands — the Cyclades
Walking in Cyprus
Walking on Malta

HIMALAYA
8000 metres
Everest: A Trekker's Guide
Trekking in the Karakoram

NORTH AMERICA
Hiking and Cycling the California Missions Trail
Hiking the Pacific Crest Trail
The John Muir Trail

SOUTH AMERICA
Aconcagua and the Southern Andes
Hiking and Biking Peru's Inca Trails
Trekking in Torres del Paine

AFRICA
Climbing Toubkal
Kilimanjaro
Walking in the Drakensberg
Walks and Scrambles in the Moroccan Anti-Atlas

NEW ZEALAND AND AUSTRALIA
Hiking the Overland Track

CHINA, JAPAN AND ASIA
Annapurna
Hiking and Trekking in the Japan Alps and Mount Fuji
Hiking in Hong Kong
Japan's Kumano Kodo Pilgrimage
Japan's Kumano Kodo Pilgrimage
Trekking in Bhutan
Trekking in Ladakh
Trekking in Tajikistan
Trekking in the Himalaya

TECHNIQUES
Fastpacking
The Mountain Hut Book

MINI GUIDES
Alpine Flowers
Navigation

MOUNTAIN LITERATURE
A Walk in the Clouds
Abode of the Gods
Fifty Years of Adventure
The Pennine Way — the Path, the People, the Journey
Unjustifiable Risk?

For full information on all our guides, books and eBooks, visit our website:
www.cicerone.co.uk

CICERONE

Trust Cicerone to guide your next adventure, wherever it may be around the world...

Discover guides for hiking, mountain walking, backpacking, trekking, trail running, cycling and mountain biking, ski touring, climbing and scrambling in Britain, Europe and worldwide.

Connect with Cicerone online and find inspiration.

- buy books and ebooks
- articles, advice and trip reports
- GPX files and updates
- regular newsletter

cicerone.co.uk